Making Peace
With Your
Teenager

Discovery House
PUBLISHERS

BOX 3566 · GRAND RAPIDS, MI 49501

*PUBLISHING BOOKS THAT FEED
THE SOUL WITH THE WORD OF GOD.*

Making Peace
With Your
Teenager

The REST Strategy

Kevin Huggins
Phil Landrum

Library of Congress Cataloging-in-Publication Data

Huggins, Kevin.
    Making peace with your teenager : the REST strategy /
Kevin Huggins, Phil Landrum.
        p. cm.
    ISBN 0–929239–71–7
    1. Parent and teenager. 2. Family—Religious life.
3. Teenagers—Religious life. 4. Parenting—Religious
aspects—Christianity. I. Landrum, Phil. II. Title.
HQ799.15.H82 1993
649'.125—dc20   93–24752
                                                          CIP

Discovery House Publishers is affiliated with Radio Bible
Class, Grand Rapids, Michigan

Discovery House books are distributed to the trade by Thomas
Nelson Publishers, Nashville, Tennessee 37214

Printed in the United States of America

96 / CHG / 10 9 8 7 6 5 4

Contents

WE DEDICATE THIS BOOK TO OUR PARENTS

To Michael and Debbie Huggins

As I had opportunity to observe my own parents and the way they responded to me at each stage of my life, I always knew there was something unusual about them. Something that put them in a position to make me feel incredibly secure and supported in their love.

As I wrote this book it was my prayer that every teen-ager could have the opportunity to experience parents who operated from the same kind of position as mine did. And still do. When parents fill a position like this in their kids' lives, they become "the pride of their children," just as the writer of Proverbs teaches (Prov. 17:6). I am proud of them. And thankful to God for the gift they have been to me.

To Clyde and Ruby Landrum

If everyone on earth had the opportunity to watch Clyde and Ruby in action, we would need very few books on parenting. They truly represent God on this planet.

Foreword

Rest.

It's a great word. Jesus talked about the importance of our being at rest. However, most parents are just the opposite. Too often we parent from a position of pressure when our children are teenagers. To make things worse, we pass this pressure along to our adolescents.

That's why the "REST Strategy" in *Making Peace With Your Teenager* is so welcome. It helps parents avoid the pressure. It helps us relax. The "REST Strategy" gives us a game plan to follow so we can enjoy those years from junior high through college.

Also, the "REST Strategy" is biblically based. Only in God's Word can we find peace. As Jesus said, "Come to me . . . and I will give you rest" (Matthew 11:28).

Parents will thank Kevin and Phil for reminding us that we can be at rest. It's welcome news.

Jay Kesler, President
Taylor University

One

Correcting Our Two Biggest Mistakes

There's a stranger in the house. It's our teenager—the kid who's always been such a delight. And last night was the last straw.

She's fifteen, and the lying has been going on for about six months now. This time the report card started the arguing, which led to the screaming, the slamming door, the sobbing— and the two hot-faced parents sitting dazed on the couch.

He's seventeen and has always been a gentleman. But that's not what the parents of his girlfriend said last night in the phone call. When his parents confronted him, he seemed insulted and growled that he had to get love someplace; he certainly doesn't get it from Mom and Dad.

She's thirteen and suddenly as unpredictable as the weather. All the rules are out the window. Last night, like every night, was a never-ending battle. A year ago she was such a great kid.

He's eighteen, and it's been three months since he started his freshman year at college. Mom and Dad thought he'd never come home. But the first night back was no fun. He wants nothing to do with them or with what they stand for. They are hypocrites. Everything they believe is a waste of time and has nothing to do with the real world.

She's sixteen and has been pushing the rules a lot lately. Last night, she was to be in by midnight. When she came home at 2:00 a.m., the place went up for grabs. Mom and Dad were screaming. She narrowed her eyes and looked at them with such hate, it chilled them. But she said nothing. They kept yelling. She just stood there. She asked if they were finished. In the silence that followed, she turned and walked out of the room.

Needed: a game plan

None of us expects to someday be at war with our teenagers. But someplace along the line, during those years between twelve and twenty, the battle lines are drawn.

What happens next to our kids and to ourselves as parents depends on whether we have a biblical game plan for working with our teens during these tough times.

Just as a successful coach must have a game plan, and a successful business must have a game plan, so also we parents must have a game plan to help us and our teenagers deal with adolescent problems.

So, where does this game plan start? First, we must recognize and eliminate the two biggest mistakes we make.

Defining problems

"My kid has problems!"

Granted. All people have problems. The only ones who don't are those who have died and gone to heaven. So it's a given that our daughters and sons are not exempt and will have problems—especially during that adolescent period.

There's a good reason why those junior high, senior high, and college years are the most acute. Something happens in that period as our sons and daughters leave childhood. William J. O'Malley was writing about his son when he so beautifully described the process that precipitates these problems:

> Here's this nice, healthy little kid, comfortable with his peers and parents, as unconcerned

about his looks as a bulldog, his awareness and focus completely outside himself.

Then, literally overnight . . . his body starts shooting out all kinds of magic potions like a werewolf at full moon. His limbs elongate and go gangly and ungovernable; his face gets fuzzy, knobby. A lot of vulpine urges start whispering into hitherto unsuspected cellars of his soul. . . .

He knows he's the same kid, but he's not the same kid at all. He's always been able to get his arms and legs to do what he wanted them to do. His voice never played such humiliating tricks on him. And other parts of his body seem to be willfully independent minds of their own, too.

If the boy's parents think they've spawned an alien changeling, how do you think the boy himself feels?

At every natural life crisis so far a child has had to face an unnerving change that opens up a new, more challenging way of being human. Birth itself is a traumatic disequilibrium, then, weaning and potty training. Then being shunted out to play with the other snotty kids. Then, the betrayal at the kindergarten doorway.

But if each of these crises was a mortar blast, adolescence is the atomic bomb. . . .

These changes are as numerous for our girls. Menstrual cramps. Rearranged figures. Acne. Breasts—or no breasts. Hair. Changing relationships with the opposite sex—and parents.

Wall-to-wall changes. And we haven't even gotten into cheer leading tryouts, varsity sports, dating pressures, studies, school work, college tests, family crises, career planning, learning to drive, or drinking and drugs.

What's a problem? What's not?

What is our role as parents in dealing with all these changes? Which of our teenager's crises should receive our attention? Which shouldn't? To answer this we need to clarify what we mean by problems that require our involvement. That's difficult because what some of us consider a problem might be considered completely incidental by others.

Debbie's dating, Doug is dateless. Should we care? Some of us think it's a big problem that our kids are dating. We worry about it night after night, weekend after weekend. Other parents feel it's a problem if our kids aren't dating. One date, Lord! Just one date for my kid!

Outgoing or shy? Some parents feel that if our kid is being honest, assertive and speaking up, claiming her rights, that's a big problem. Then, some of us have kids who are quiet, shy and compliant, never expressing their opinions and we fear that's a problem.

Beautiful Barbara or unkempt Kenny? Often we feel it's a problem if our teenagers are too attractive or too popular at school. We fear that their friends have too much influence in their lives. Conversely, many parents of kids who are unattractive and not very popular fear that is a problem. We wonder if something is wrong with their personalities.

Which is it? Is too little dating or too much dating a problem? Should we want our teenagers to be assertive or non-assertive? Is being always with other kids or always being alone the problem?

Thirteen-year-old on strike

For two days I looked forward to a lunch date with my family. I figured my daughters were excited, too. The date was set several days in advance. But when it came time to go, my thirteen-year-old went on strike!

No explanation. No logic. Just, "I don't want to go. I'd rather stay home."

What should I do? Sit down and discuss it at length and make everyone else wait? Ignore it and let her stay home? Have a showdown and make her go?

Is it a problem that she doesn't want to go with the family? If it is a problem, what kind of solution should I be shooting for?

How do parents make these kinds of judgment calls? First, we have to decide if something is really a problem, or not. Does it even need solving? If it is a problem, then we have to decide how on earth to solve it. What is an appropriate solution to such a situation? We're constantly bombarded with this matter of solving problems.

What do you consider a problem? This is a key question because what we define as a problem determines where the majority of our parenting time is spent. We focus most of our time and energy on trying to solve the problems in our kids' lives, don't we? One mother said, "I'm so busy solving my three teenagers' problems that I hardly have any time for myself. They just have one problem after another. I don't know how parents of teenagers have enough hours in the day to meet their kids' needs, let alone their own."

A wise parent is going to consider, Wait a minute. Rather than using all my time trying to solve every crisis that arises in my kid's life, I have to be more selective and carefully define what really is a problem that requires my parental involvement.

So how do we make this call?

The answer won't come from a psychologist, a man-made philosophy, a school, or some local, national, or world-wide government.

To be effective, the answer must come from a source other than the latest fad touted by the experts. Fad parenting is doomed because it is based on cultural conditions and values that change from one generation to the other and from one geographic region to another.

We need a guide to parenting that is relevant to every culture and every generation. We believe the answer can only come from God; therefore, our parenting strategy must be based on principles found in His guidebook for life, the Bible. The strategy we will describe and advocate is based on the Bible as the authority.

How does the Bible define what is truly a problem in a teenager's life? What does the Bible say should be the priority for a parent's time and energies?

Let's turn to the New Testament, to Galatians, a letter written by perhaps the most famous of Jesus Christ's disciples, the Apostle Paul.

Paul had a parent-like relationship with a group of Christians who lived in the Roman province of Galatia. He refers to them as "my dear children, for whom I am again in the pains of childbirth" (Gal. 4:19).

The Galatians had some serious problems. Paul had started this church. He nurtured these folks while they were still young in their faith and showed them how God wanted them to live. Then he moved on to start other churches. Back in Galatia, some false teachers rushed in and got people off track. Paul wrote back to his children, "You were running a good race. Who cut in on you and kept you from obeying the truth? That kind of persuasion does not come from the one who calls you" (Gal. 5:7–8).

Sounds like something a parent of a teenager might write. Who's influencing my kids? I never taught them to act that way! Where'd they learn to do that?

A real problem is. . .

Notice how Paul, acting as a parent, defines a problem. He said a real problem is someone or something that persuades our children to get off the path God lays out for them in the Bible. Paul's definition of a problem here in Galatians is the definition we recommend parents use.

According to Paul, the problems on which we parents need to focus our attention are any event, relationship, or behavior that persuades or threatens to persuade our kids to live outside the boundaries God gives in the Bible.

Out of love for us God established moral boundaries to guide human beings toward productive and meaningful lives. He revealed these to us in the Bible. From now on in this book when we refer to boundaries, we'll call them *God's pathway* or the *track of truth*.

Any event, relationship, or behavior that persuades our kids to move off the track of truth, or go off the path God has laid out for them to travel, is a serious problem. It's serious because living outside of God's moral boundaries destroys an adolescent's wholeness, that is, her productivity for God, her life of usefulness and service to God, and eventually her capacity to even love and have meaningful relationships. Remember, too, that kids can get off the pathway in two ways.

They can get off outwardly by choosing an action that God forbids. Or they can get off inwardly by choosing an action for evil or selfish purposes. Kids may appear to be on the track outwardly, while inwardly they are way off track. God is always more concerned with who a person is inwardly rather than with what she is outwardly.

It's interesting how Paul uses the word *persuasion*. That word carries pressure with it. In our world today many events, relationships, and people are trying to convince our kids—to pressure them—to take a different path to happiness or fulfillment than the one God prescribes.

In using as the definition of a problem, "any event, relationship, or behavior that persuades or threatens to persuade our kids to leave the track of truth," we're assuming parents are familiar with the track themselves and have made it clear to their kids.

It's our job to show our kids where the path is, through our example, our words, and our rules. When something or someone then comes along and attempts to persuade them to get off the track, it's time for parental intervention. The older our kids grow the greater the pressure will be on them to move outside God's moral boundaries in handling life and finding fulfillment.

It's not so hard controlling this pressure when they are young. How many people are persuading them to go outside God's moral boundaries when they are three? How much access do they have to others who might influence them? Maybe a few people in the nursery school, at church, a couple kids in the neighborhood, somebody in the family. That's somewhat controllable, isn't it?

At five they head off to the school classroom. Now there are a bunch of other people to persuade our children to get off the track of truth.

What happens when there are four kindergartners at the table and only three crayons? The children sit there watching each other, learning from each other. They soon learn that when there are four people and only three crayons, you hit somebody. Then, you grab the crayon out of her hand. When she tries to grab it back, you push her out of the chair.

What has my child just learned? When there's not enough of something, you move outside of God's moral boundaries to solve that quandary.

Our son or daughter can be persuaded to get off God's pathway as other children model the wrong way to deal with such issues.

The older children grow, the more people there are bombarding them, teaching them new ways—often the wrong ways—to handle life's challenges. Counteracting these false teachers becomes a greater and greater task to parents. It's important we avoid two big mistakes.

First mistake: distracted from the real problem

We parents easily get tied up trying to solve things that really aren't problems at all. Sometimes we try to eliminate anything in our kids' lives that makes us feel unpleasant.

For example, a thirteen-year-old boy leaves for school in the morning with his bedroom messy. Mom and Dad walk by his room and look in. The sight of a messy bedroom certainly triggers unpleasant emotions! However, unless that messy bedroom represents a willful decision on the part of their son to live outside God's moral boundaries, it's not the kind of problem that should take a lot of energy. Treating situations like these as serious problems takes away from our time to deal with the events, relationships, or behaviors that pose a much greater risk of persuading our kids to move off the track of truth. Paul said, who's cut in on you? What's causing you to get off the track of truth? This was the issue for which Paul reserved the bulk of his parental time and energy.

To be biblical parents, we must develop this same ability to focus our time and energies on the real threats to our kids' safety and wholeness. Without this ability, it becomes quite difficult to keep our sanity as they move from childhood to adolescence.

Let's say our son of twelve years old, almost an adolescent, is diagnosed as having a learning disability which means that some types of learning, some types of school activities, are going to come hard for him.

Is this a problem? No. Not in and of itself. It doesn't mean that he is necessarily going to move outside of God's moral boundaries in the way he handles his learning disabilities.

However, if I find out that he believes that the only way he can get attention at school is by being the class clown, by joking and goofing off all the time, then it does become a problem. He is dealing with an insecurity by going outside God's boundaries and disrupting the class—not concentrating on the tasks that have been assigned to him. So we've got a problem, something with which we, his parents, should help him cope.

Or how about a fourteen-year-old girl who is interested in boys? Is that a problem? The fact that she has an interest in boys does not automatically mean that she is going to go outside of God's moral boundaries to pursue it.

However, if this same fourteen-year-old is pressured by a seventeen-year-old boy to sneak out at night to meet him, then we do have a problem. He's persuading her to go outside of God's moral boundaries. That's a problem that requires parental involvement.

Think of another situation. A teacher at school has made it clear that she doesn't like my son. Is that a problem? Is that enough of a reason to take my child out of that school and put him in another school? Not necessarily. My son is going to be surrounded with people throughout his life who don't like him. It doesn't become a problem unless he responds to the teacher by going outside God's moral boundaries, for example, by active or passive aggression.

We've got to be careful what we define as problems. There are many incidents and situations that don't deserve our energies because they aren't genuine problems. If we start giving time and energy to all of them, we're either going to be pulled in a million different directions, or we're not going to have enough energy left to deal with the significant problems.

When we learn what to correctly define as problems, we can concentrate on avoiding the second big mistake parents make.

Learning from Samson

Remember Samson, the strongest man who ever lived? Samson's parents faced the same challenge in raising him we face today in raising our kids.

How do we raise kids committed to living for God in a world committed to living against Him? Notice what we read about the world in which Samson was raised, as described in Judges 13:1–8:

> Again the Israelites did evil in the eyes of the Lord, so the LORD delivered them into the hands of the Philistines for forty years.
>
> A certain man of Zorah, named Manoah, from the clan of Danites, had a wife who was sterile and remained childless. The angel of the LORD appeared to her and said: "You are sterile and childless, but you are going to conceive and have a son. Now see to it that you drink no wine or other fermented drink and that you do not eat anything unclean, because you will conceive and give birth to a son. No razor may be used on his head, because the boy is to be a Nazirite, set apart to God from birth, and he will begin the deliverance of Israel from the hands of the Philistines."
>
> Then the woman went to her husband and told him, "A man of God came to me. He looked like an angel of God, very awesome. I didn't ask him where he came from, and he didn't tell me his name. But he said to me, 'You will conceive and give birth to a son. Now then, drink no wine or other fermented drink and do not eat anything unclean, because the boy will be a Nazirite of God from birth until the day of his death.' "
>
> Then Manoah prayed to the LORD: "O Lord, I beg you, let the man of God you sent to us come

again to teach us how to bring up the boy who is to be born."

These parents were given the task of raising their son in a world hostile toward God, a world hostile to anyone who was trying to live on the track of truth.

No wonder Samson's parents greeted the news that they were going to have a son with such apprehension.

They started out very fearful about the whole task of parenting. And the closer Samson got to adolescence, the more terrified they felt—not unlike how we feel with our kids. This is why Manoah asked God for a no-fail approach or formula for parenting Samson.

Manoah felt a lot of pressure to raise his son without making any mistakes. That was his big mistake. When we take on this same pressure, we make the same mistake he did.

At the end of Judges 13 there is a curious verse. It says about Samson that "the Spirit of the LORD began to stir him." It goes from that statement right into chapter 14, which opens saying that Samson went to Timnah, where he saw a Philistine woman. And he returned to his father and mother and said, "I have seen a Philistine woman in Timnah; now get her for me as my wife" (14:1–2).

Samson was forbidden by God's commands to marry a Philistine woman. What's going on with him? Is it possible that a kid who is being stirred by the Holy Spirit could behave in this defiant and disrespectful way?

Yes. The Spirit of God often uses all the changes that come with adolescence to get kids stirred up, to get them unsettled, to get them thinking, There's got to be more to life—something that's going to satisfy me on a deeper level.

God wants teenagers asking questions and wrestling with the meaning of life, questions like: Does life really consist of the status quo? Or is there something more or better to life? Adolescence gets kids confronting these questions.

During this time it's important that their moms and dads are there to help them look for answers within God's moral boundaries.

As our kids, stirred by all the changes of adolescence, look for meaning and satisfaction, often they assume these can only be found outside of God's moral boundaries, off the path God has laid out—sexual relationships, drugs, making big bucks illegally.

When they start to go outside God's moral boundaries to find life, as Samson did, they need their parents to step in and guide them back on the path. That's a big part of what it means to help solve kids' problems.

But what did Manoah and his wife do? When Samson laid down the law, telling them to get that Philistine girl for him, they replied, "Isn't there an acceptable woman among your relatives or among all our people? Must you go to the uncircumcised Philistines to get a wife?" (14:3).

Don't they sound desperate? They were not acting as the strong, stable figures that their teen needed them to be, but were weak and unstable.

Samson's parents were in a position of weakness. We don't sense anything in them that reflects peace, rest, or strength. We see stress, pressure, and fear. How did they respond when they parented from this position?

First, they pleaded with Samson not to go out of God's moral boundaries. When he resisted, they ended up helping him find satisfaction down the wrong path.

They went down to Timnah and helped him get that girl for his wife.

They made a big mistake—a mistake that ultimately robbed them of their leadership role in their family.

What was that mistake? They responded to their son's problem from the wrong position—a position of pressure that led to weakness and compromise.

Samson's parents felt pressure to control their child and make him into the certain kind of person they thought God wanted him to be.

That doesn't sound like such an unhealthy position for a parent, does it? It sounds like a concerned parent. It sounds like a loving parent. But let's take a closer look to see the true nature of this kind of parenting. When we respond to our teens from this position we usually choose one of two strategies.

Strategy #1—Intimidation

This is what Manoah and his wife used first.

Intimidation usually involves using some kind of pain to control our kid and modify her behavior: I'm going to make it so painful for you if you ever do that again! Understand me? Do you?

We yell loud. We threaten. We take away privileges. We enforce consequences. The goal behind this strategy is to control outward behavior.

Strategy #2—Bargaining

If the main tool of the intimidating parent is pain, the main tool of the bargaining parent is pleasure. Parents coax their adolescents to behave by providing various forms of pleasure to them.

One dad did his best to intimidate his daughter, Marcie, into being a "good Christian girl," to go to the church youth group, to hang around with the right kids, to get good grades.

The more this dad threatened, screamed, and took things away, the more Marcie demonstrated that she was going to do what she pleased. The dad started thinking, Wait a minute! I'm using the wrong strategy. I've got to start using psychology on this kid. So he switched to bargaining.

He bought a Corvette, and he called it, "Marcie's Motivation Car." Dad drove the 'vette to work Monday through

Friday. But on Saturday and Sunday Marcie could drive the car if she stayed within the boundaries prescribed for her all week. Fantastic pleasure could be hers if she would just be a good girl. That's bargaining.

Samson's parents also used this strategy. They tried to intimidate him by pleading, yelling, jumping up and down, and pulling their hair out. It didn't work, so they started bargaining.

"OK. We'll go down and get this bride. You bring her back up here to Israel. But then you must start behaving. We don't want any more of this running around, partying stuff. Getting married should settle you down." What they were saying is: We'll give you a little pleasure as a way to keep you under control.

Why, as in the case of Samson, do the strategies of intimidating or bargaining ultimately backfire on parents?

They backfire because all they do is get the kids to temporarily modify their behavior outwardly, but they do nothing to affect changes in their hearts.

As long as we keep up the pain, our kids stay in the boundaries. What happens when we're not around to produce the pain? Whoops! Back outside the boundaries they go!

Or they'll stick around as long as we're inventing new pleasures for them. However, pleasures are subject to the law of diminishing returns. The pleasures that kept them on track this summer are not going to work next summer.

This summer sending her with her friends to an amusement park was enough. She was twelve. What about when she's thirteen? You're going to have to buy her a mini-bike, roller blades, and bankroll her to go to any movie she wants.

That's thirteen. What do you think you'll have to do at fourteen? By the time she is a sophomore in high school, you're going to have to send her to Europe! You have to continue increasing the pleasure in order to keep her from wandering off the path.

Let's go back to the assumption parents make who use these two strategies, intimidation and bargaining: It's *my* responsibility to do whatever I can do to keep this kid inside these boundaries. *I've* got to do it. It's *my* job.

That's why we call this parenting under pressure, or parenting from stress.

Second mistake: parenting under pressure

That's the second mistake parents make: when our kids start having problems by getting off the track of truth we respond from a position of pressure.

We call this "parenting under pressure" because not only does the kid feel pressure—whether we give her pain or pleasure, it's pressure to be the kind of kid you want her to be—we feel pressure, as well, to be the kind of parents who keep our kids perfectly behaved, perfectly satisfied, perfectly packaged. We say to ourselves, I've got to come up with something! Got to go to another seminar! Got to read another book! Got to talk to somebody! Got to find a parent who's got a perfect kid! Got to do something to make this kid come out right!

There is no sense of peace, just pressure and stress. The parent feels pressure; the kid feels pressure.

The only way we can feel peace is to distance ourselves from our teen, not be around her. At least for a while we have that kid out of our presence. And what about her? When can she feel at peace?

When she's in our presence there's so much pressure she feels forced either to resist, or to pretend to go along with us. Neither of these enhance a relationship. Our kids want to get away from us, too.

The most important task of adolescence

The most important task facing our kids during adolescence is to decide what kind of people they are going to be for the rest of their lives.

When we operate from a position of pressure we try to take responsibility for that decision away from them and try to decide for them. Our kids hear us saying: *I* will tell you what kind of person you're going to be! Do you understand? You sit at *my* table. You eat *my* food. *I'm* paying for your college education. *I* buy your clothes. *I* pay your transportation. That gives *me* the right to tell you what kind of person you're going to be!

Do parents have that right? I think God would say no. He has given each teen that right. No matter what we do for our children, we can't take that right away from them. It's their God-given decision. In their hearts they know it. And they will resent us if we try to take away from them the right to decide what kind of persons they want to be. That's theirs!

When we try to make this decision for them, they feel it immediately. Mom, Dad, you're trying to tell me what kind of person I have to be. That's my decision to make! I'll show you that you can't make me into what you want.

This creates a power struggle and we end up losing control and influence in their lives instead of gaining it.

There is an alternative to parenting under pressure. The Bible describes a position that is radically different—a position that, once discovered, transforms the whole way parents approach their kids—parenting from a position of rest.

The answer: parenting at rest

Isn't that an appealing word—*rest*. If you're a parent of a teenager, I've got a feeling that word sounds really good to you.

Rest. God calls us to parent from a position of rest, not from a position of pressure.

Remember the underlying assumption of the position of pressure? It's my responsibility to control my kid, to keep my kid from moving outside God's moral boundaries, to tell her what kind of person she's going to be. It's my responsibility to do that.

That generates a ton of pressure. But what's the assumption that parents at rest make?

Although I care deeply about the kind of person my kid decides to be, I can't control how she makes that decision. I don't need to because, ultimately, God is in control.

There's a world of difference between these two positions, parenting under pressure and parenting at rest.

Parenting under pressure sets me up to be hostile toward my teen because I'm trying to control the kind of person she is. Parenting at rest frees me to be an ally to my teen because I'm giving her resources to decide what kind of person she wants to be.

We looked at parents—Manoah and his wife—under pressure. Now, let's turn to the New Testament and observe Paul again. Remember the parent-like relationship he had with the Galatians? He had the same kind of parental relationship with the people in Thessalonica. Read 1 Thessalonians 2:6–13:

> We were not looking for praise from men, not from you or anyone else.
>
> As apostles of Christ we could have been a burden to you, but we were gentle among you, like a mother caring for her little children. We loved you so much that we were delighted to share with you not only the gospel of God but our lives as well, because you had become so dear to us. Surely you remember, brothers, our toil and hard-

ship; we worked night and day in order not to be a burden to anyone while we preached the gospel of God to you.

You are witnesses, and so is God, of how holy, righteous and blameless we were among you who believed. For you know that we dealt with each of you as a father deals with his own children, encouraging, comforting and urging you to live lives worthy of God, who calls you into his kingdom and glory.

And we also thank God continually because, when you received the word of God, which you heard from us, you accepted it not as the word of men, but as it actually is, the word of God, which is at work in you who believe.

Notice the words Paul used, such words as *delighted* and *dear*. Paul enjoyed parenting because he wasn't parenting from pressure.

Parenting at rest is active

It is important to note here that parenting from a position of rest is not parenting in an apathetic, complacent, or lazy manner. That is the danger of using the word *rest*, I suppose.

In this passage, it's obvious that Paul worked hard. He reminded his readers of his toil and hardship on their behalf. He said he worked night and day for them.

Parenting at rest is an active style of parenting. It is a style of parenting in which lots of energy is expended, but in fundamentally different ways than when parenting under pressure.

That's the key. If we parent from pressure we really don't believe God is at work in our kids' lives. We really believe we have to do it ourselves. We believe that Christian maturity somehow comes from us working from the outside in.

Parenting at rest takes the pressure off us

However, if we're parenting from a position of rest we believe maturity depends upon God working in our kids' lives from the inside out.

When we understand that the God who created the universe loves our child and is calling her to live within His boundaries of moral truth, we can step back and rest, and say, I wonder how I can cooperate with this. That's why Paul said, I thank God continually because when you received the Word of God from us, you accepted it not as the word of man, but as it actually is, the Word of God, which is at work in you.

Paul realized the only way the Thessalonians were going to become the people God wanted them to be was by God doing a work in their hearts. It's not something that he, by using pressure from the outside, could accomplish. That's why he thanked God instead of patting himself on the back. Only God can change a human heart.

For parents, that takes a ton of pressure off. We're not pressuring ourselves to control what we can't control. As much as we might try to fool our teens or even fool ourselves into believing that we can control the kind of persons they become, we can't.

Parenting at rest takes pressure off teens

Parenting at rest also takes a ton of pressure off our teen. Who she chooses to be is an issue now between her and God. Whatever she decides, we are committed to loving her and staying involved with her. We haven't made our love conditional on how she makes that decision.

Parenting at rest puts pressure on God

When we parent at rest all the pressure that we normally put on ourselves and our kids is placed somewhere else. It's placed on God, where it belongs. He's the only one who has broad enough shoulders and a strong enough back to assume the responsibility for our kids.

The big difference between parents under pressure and parents at rest is where we're leaning our weight. Parents at stress are leaning all the weight on themselves and their kids. Parents at rest have shifted the weight onto the Lord.

When I am at rest I know it's up to God to do a work in my kid's life. I can't move her heart onto the track of truth, using pain or using pleasure. That's a work that God's Spirit must do.

What I can do is to get on the track myself and show how great it is for me, how much I enjoy it. I can urge her to follow the path with me. But there's no way I can make her follow it. That's going to have to be a work of God.

A scary experience

One of the scariest experiences I ever had as a parent occurred a few years ago when my oldest daughter and I were returning from church together. She was halfway through seventh grade at the time. As we were driving home I asked, "How did Sunday school go?" I had just hired a new junior high pastor at our church. I wanted to find out if this guy was doing a good job.

"Well, it was okay." That wasn't exactly what I wanted to hear.

"What did he talk about?"

"Oh . . . something about the fact that we ought to be reading and studying the Bible on our own." There was something less than enthusiasm in her voice.

"Well, what do you think of that idea?" She paused and gulped as if to say, I don't know if Dad's ready to hear this. But she said it to me anyway.

"I think it's just a waste of time."

Aaagh! But, before I could say anything, she continued.

"How do we know that God really wrote the Bible? How do we know if He even exists? Seems like it's a big waste of time."

At that moment I felt sheer terror. For the first time it hit me that my child could actually choose to be an unbeliever. She'd made all the decisions in children's church, camp, VBS. But here she was now as a teenager confessing some pretty strong doubts. And suddenly I felt so much pressure to stop the car, reach over, and shake her until she said, "I recant. I believe, I'll read the Bible." That would have been using pain to get her to outwardly walk the direction I wanted her to walk.

What would that have accomplished? It wouldn't have moved her heart onto the track of truth. For a fact, it would have made her heart more committed to stay away from it. Also, it would have made her more committed to never let me know where her heart really is, because it would be too dangerous to be honest with Dad again. A parent under pressure forces his kids to pretend or to avoid him.

But in that moment, God's Spirit gave me the strength to somehow keep all my pressure inside. I thought I was going to explode. I couldn't wait to get home. I went into the study, shut the door, and began to cry out to God.

"God . . . what in the world is going on here? If this girl runs off and becomes a prodigal, who are they going to blame? They're not going to blame You, God. They're going to blame me, the dad. So it's my reputation that's at stake, Lord, not Yours. It's my responsibility."

That's how I was feeling that moment, but something about it seemed unhealthy to me. I decided not to discuss it further with my daughter until I felt more at rest—until I could get away from feeling so much pressure. It took me several hours of praying until I finally could say, "OK, God, this girl is your responsibility. I realize I can't make her believe. I could put pressure on her, but it's just going to hurt her. I can't make her believe. I don't know what I'm supposed to do right now as a parent, but I feel like I need to stay involved with this girl. That's all I know."

So I went up to her room and sat down on the edge of her bed and said, "I want to talk to you more about the topic you brought up in the car today." She looked at me as if to say, This is a prelude to a lecture, isn't it, Dad? I could read it in her eyes. However, I felt no pressure to lecture her. I just wanted to invite her to talk more about her doubts and questions.

To this day, I really don't remember much of what was said in that conversation. But I do remember trying to communicate to her that it was safe to express her doubts to me. It was safe and I was interested and concerned.

I remember feeling both unsettled and at rest at the same time. Uncertain about what would happen, but at rest with the fact it was out of my hands. It was between her and God.

For a couple months not a lot more was said, until one day she came into my study and made a request.

"Dad, do you have a Bible with the books in the chronological order that they were written?"

"Yeah." I pulled one off my shelf and gave it to her. "Why are you asking for that?"

"Well, you know when I told you a couple months ago that I wasn't sure about the Bible, and maybe God didn't really write it?"

"Yeah."

"Well, one thing you said to me then was that I shouldn't make up my mind about it until I read it through for myself. So that's what I've decided I'm going to do this summer. And anytime I find something that I don't understand I'm going to ask you. It's going to be your job to explain it to me."

That blew me away. I didn't remember saying it. But God's Spirit had given me that sentence to say in the midst of my fog and confusion. Over the summer we had a number of meaningful conversations on different parts of the Bible, and I was able to help her understand them. That was the beginning of a two-year process; at the end of it she came to me and said, "Dad, I want to turn my life over to Christ."

I don't think I had much to do with the outcome. But that's the genius of parenting from a position of rest. The key thing that I did was that I didn't pressure her. Somehow God helped me move to a position of rest, even though I felt unsettled about it. At the same time, I felt at rest because God was overseeing this.

I thought that would be the hardest problem I would ever have to face.

But that was just preparation for a harder problem which came later, which in turn prepared me for a still more difficult problem. With each problem, the shift had to happen over again. Learning to make this shift from self-reliance to reliance on God is perhaps the most important thing a parent can do.

Two

Making the Choice:
Compliance or Compassion?

It was a hot summer day, but in the fitness center it was even hotter in the steam room. Almost hidden by the steam, two businessmen were talking in generalities.

"Well, how's it going?"

"I don't know what I'm going to do with my son Kyle. I mean, I just about killed that boy this weekend!"

"What happened?"

"I'd been telling him not to buy fireworks, not to set them off. It's against the law. But he went out and bought some without my knowing. And when we were gone for a few hours Saturday, he set off all these fireworks in our back yard, near our neighbors' house.

Back yard fireworks

"Soon the smoke bombs, firecrackers, and rockets produced all this smoke, which went into our neighbor's air conditioning unit. When the air conditioner sucked all the smoke in our neighbor thought his house was on fire, so he called the fire department. Pretty soon, two or three fire trucks came roaring up to their house. The firemen searched the whole house and were about to take hatchets to the walls, when they realized the smoke was coming from our backyard.

"Now I'm going to have to pay to completely repaint my neighbor's house because of smoke damage. And they're billing me five hundred dollars for the fire trucks to come out on a false alarm.

"I just don't know what I'm going to do with my son. Do you have any suggestions?"

"Boy! I know what I'd do with him! If he were my kid I'd beat the tar out of him. He'd be too scared to ever try something like that again."

Imagine if that's the guidance we were given. Go home and beat the tar out of our kid, or in some other forceful manner pressure him so that he behaves.

That advice represents one approach to our teens' problems: get them so afraid of us they wouldn't dare go outside any boundaries we've set for them.

But let me tell you about a different approach, which another dad used.

Henry's son goes to college

Henry became quite concerned about his son Jeremy, a freshman in college. At Thanksgiving break Henry and Jeremy were talking. It became obvious to the father that his son didn't have a personal relationship with Christ. As he listened to Jeremy, Henry wondered what he should do. He's been a good kid his whole life, thought Henry. He's kept all the rules. He's been an athlete, student body president. He's never given us any problems. How does a good kid like him come to the point of seeing that he has need for a Savior? How does a good kid come to the conclusion that he shouldn't try to run his own life?

Although Henry knew that as a small boy his son had accepted Christ as his personal Savior, he wondered if Jeremy's goodness flowed out of his relationship with Christ, or out of pride and ambition. His goodness had always worked well for him and achieved for him many rewards.

When the weekend was over, Henry began to pray specifically that some event would come along in his son's life that would shatter Jeremy's illusion of his own goodness, and drive him to experience true dependence on Christ.

In essence, this father was praying for a problem to enter his son's life. He prayed that God would show Jeremy that his heart was selfish and proud even though his behavior looked Christian.

Months went by as Henry continued to pray. Then, during the boy's sophomore year, the father received a call one afternoon at work. It was the dean of the college his son attended.

"I don't know how to tell you this," said the dean. "But Jeremy has just been suspended from school because he was found using drugs with some of his friends. You'll have to come and take him home because he's been suspended for three weeks."

If Henry hadn't been praying for a problem, he would have been completely blown away by this development. Instead, as he hung up the phone, he felt thankful. *Lord, could this be it? Could this be the event I've been praying for? The event that will finally get Jeremy to realize that, despite the fact that he's been a good kid all these years, he still needs the Lord Jesus Christ to change him from the inside out?*

Henry drove to the college to pick up his son. On the way, he began to pray and to think, *How should I approach my son when I see him?*

He could have decided to beat the tar out of Jeremy. He could have yelled, "If you ever embarrass me like this again, ever get involved in drugs, I'll beat you within an inch of your life!" Instead, as he drove, Henry decided on a wholly different approach: *The main thing I want Jeremy to know is that despite what he's done, I love him and God loves him. I want to give him a taste of God's grace and forgiveness as I walk in that door.*

When Henry arrived at the campus, he walked to his son's room. There at the desk sat Jeremy, waiting for him, feeling so much shame he couldn't even look his dad in the eyes.

Henry went over and threw his arms around him. The kid melted in his arms. It was the first time Henry had ever seen any serious expression of emotion from his son. That opened the door for this kid. For the first time, Jeremy experienced God's grace. The reunion in that room began a series of conversations that resulted in this young man beginning a personal relationship with Christ. He finally found out what Christ meant when He said, "I have not come to call the righteous, but sinners" (Matt. 9:13).

Two approaches: compliance vs. compassion

These two stories depict different approaches to parenting our kids. The first approach says, I'm going to scare my kid so badly that he'll never cause me any problems. The second says, I'm going to pray for the kind of problems that will move this kid's heart toward God.

Let's examine each of these two approaches in more detail.

Remember in the last chapter how we discovered from the Bible what kind of problems really deserve our attention as parents? They were defined as "any events, relationships or emotions that persuade our teens to move off God's track of truth."

When a kid moves off God's pathway we can count on four things being true

It's not just a phase.
First, when a kid moves off God's track of truth, that is, when he starts to behave in unbiblical ways, we know that its

not just a harmless phase that he will grow out of on his own.

We've heard many psychologists and so-called experts encourage parents to view adolescence as a harmless stage: Boys will be boys! Girls just want to have fun! Let kids sow a little wild oats during this time. There's nothing we can do to prevent it anyway. They'll grow out of it.

The problem with this viewpoint is that immoral adolescents become immoral adults. It's hard to change. Whenever a kid begins to violate God's moral boundaries and live in ways that violate God's moral standards, it's not harmless. It's not true he'll grow out of it on his own. It's just a phase is a myth.

It is the teen's choice.

The second thing we know when a kid goes outside God's circle of truth is that the adolescent himself is choosing to mishandle an event, or relationship, or emotion. In most cases—there are a few exceptions—no one is threatening him with physical violence to make him lie, steal, sell drugs, or cheat. Normally, it's the teen's choice.

Choice reflects the fact that on some level this kid believes his interest is better served off the track of God's truth than on it. This decision reflects a belief, a conviction.

Thus we're dealing with more than just the behavior. Underneath the behavior there is a conviction that is leading to personal choice.

The teen needs our help.

The third thing we know when our teens go off God's pathway is that some kind of parental intervention is important and desirable. It's our moral responsibility before God. We should never abandon our teens to following their own paths: Ho, hum. I told him not to do it. Now, what can I do? He'll just have to learn his lesson the hard way.

Wrong! There should be intervention for the kid's sake and for God's sake whenever God's boundaries are violated.

Parents can make things worse.

The fourth thing we know when our kids go off the track of truth is that we can respond in ways that will just make things worse. We know there are some things that we might do to intervene that will drive them off the pathway even more, rather than encourage them to go back to the right way. This kind of intervention is destructive and detrimental.

When a problem hits, seldom have we parents planned in advance what approach we'll use. Our first instinct is to respond in a beat-the-tar- out-of-him manner. This approach doesn't make our kid want to obey God. Instead, it only increases his determination to move off God's track.

Pharisees vs. Jesus

In Matthew 9, there is recorded a conversation between Jesus and the Pharisees. The Pharisees were masters of the beat-the-tar-out-of-them approach. They were masters of using intimidation to make people comply to God's laws. In verse 9, "Jesus saw a man named Matthew sitting at the tax collector's booth."

In the days of the New Testament, tax collectors operated outside God's pathway. They were dishonest and corrupt.

Notice that Jesus didn't write off Matthew. Instead He said to him, "Follow me." He invited him to spend time with Him.

Much to the shock of the Pharisees, Matthew got up and followed Him. Later, when Jesus was having dinner at Matthew's house, a number of other tax collectors came and ate with Jesus and His disciples.

The Pharisees who saw this asked Jesus' disciples, "Why does your teacher eat with tax collectors and 'sinners?'" (v. 11). In other words, Why does your teacher prefer to hang out with those guys rather than with us?

It didn't make sense that this great teacher from God

would be more interested in people who were living outside the Law than in those living within it.

Jesus overheard this and answered with a principle that guided His whole approach to people. "It is not the healthy who need a doctor, but the sick" (v. 12). If Jesus used a family analogy instead of a medical one, He might say it this way: It's not the healthy kids who need parents; it's sick ones.

Too often we are shocked when our kids get to adolescence. All of a sudden they declare independence and begin to act out what's been inside all along. They show some of their ugly parts. Puzzled, we think, I thought if a kid grew up *in our home*, he wouldn't be sick spiritually.

But wait a minute! Don't forget what the Bible teaches about human nature. All kids, no matter what home they come out of, are going to be spiritually sick. That's why God gave them parents, right? If they didn't have problems they wouldn't need parents. That's what Jesus meant when He told the Pharisees it's not the healthy ones who need a doctor. That's why every parent should be prepared for problems. But Jesus wasn't through yet. In the next sentence, He gave the Pharisees a second reason why He approached people the way He did: "I desire mercy, not sacrifice" (v. 13).

The word *mercy* is a very strong word used many places in Scripture, and is also translated as "loyalty" or "compassion." It's a word that pictures one hundred percent uncoerced, voluntary love.

I desire voluntary love, not sacrifice, He said.

The word here translated "sacrifice" is used in the Scriptures to convey the idea of dutiful compliance—the exact opposite of voluntary love—one hundred percent coerced conformity of behavior.

So what was Jesus saying? He meant, If you guys want to know why I hang out with this group of people—the tax collectors—instead of this group of people—the Pharisees—

go and learn what this means: I desire compassion, not compliance.

There are two distinct approaches represented by these words. The Pharisees called people to compliance, in contrast to Christ, who called people to compassion.

Imagine that our teen has gone off God's track of truth. And he's living out there. We know that intervention by us, his parents, is important.

We can intervene in one of two ways. We can approach him like the Pharisees, and call him to compliance, or we can approach him like Jesus, and call him to compassion. Although the outer behavior of each approach may at times appear very similar, the attitude and impact of each approach will be very different.

Remember the beat-the-tar-out-of-the-kid approach? That's the approach that calls for dutiful compliance. Jesus, however, said that we should approach our teens with compassion, instead—just as Henry prayed that Jeremy would learn to love Christ.

The call to compliance

This was the approach of the Pharisees. It was my approach when I first got involved in youth work. I was going to call the kids in my church back onto God's pathway, and I was going to do it by calling them to compliance.

The impact I had on the kids in that church was destructive. The louder I issued my call the more determined these kids were to go the opposite direction.

About six months into that year, a few of the moms came to me and said, "There's something about your approach that's driving our kids away from church, and we feel it's driving our kids away from the Lord. We wish you would think about it, because we don't feel like its getting to the kids' hearts at all."

The call to compassion

That's when I realized there had to be a better way of approaching kids, an approach that calls them to something more than behavioral compliance; an approach that calls them to give their hearts to a cause; an approach that calls them to love someone or something other than themselves. Kids usually have a far better response to a call like this than they do to a call just to conform.

When our kids get off God's track of truth, it's wrong not to call them back. But the approach we take in calling them back onto that pathway is critical. Our approach is much more important than our specific behaviors or words.

That's why some parents can be effective even without a whole lot of creativity and intelligence, or without the benefit of a good youth group or a good youth pastor, or without talent in counseling. They may be a bit clumsy as they respond. But they're effective, because they're calling their kids to compassion.

These parents are more effective than parents who have had the benefit of all the seminars, books, counselors, and education about parenting—but who are calling their kids to compliance

The basic problem most of us are up against is not a lack of skill or knowledge. The problem is we use the wrong approach. We call kids to compliance, instead of to compassion.

The advantages of compassion

The focus of the call to compassion is on the teen's heart, instead of on the teen's behavior.

When we're parenting with a call to compliance we focus only on our teen's behavior. That's all we can see and that's all we care about.

This is true even in the business world. When businesses only focus on making workers comply, often they completely ignore what the workers think or feel. Businesses where management focuses on what employees are thinking and feeling are more able to inspire employee dedication and excellence.

If what we want from our kids is not just half-hearted conformity, but whole-hearted obedience, then it is necessary to focus on what they are feeling inwardly. What is it that they kids are really after? What are they shooting for? What are they trying to accomplish? These questions focus on the teens' hearts, not on their behavior.

When I started using this approach as a youth pastor, I discovered that the first thing I had to do was to get to know the kids in my youth group. I had to find out not only what they were doing but what they were thinking and feeling.

We don't have to know people at all to call them to compliance. But it's impossible to call them to compassion without getting to know them intimately. What we're trying to do is to get our children to bend their hearts, not just bend their knees. That requires developing personal relationships with them.

When we call our teens to compassion, our behaviors involve teaching, not manipulation.

The one thing that God calls every parent to do is to teach. God does not call us to control our kids' behavior, but He calls us to teach our kids. Very few parents make it their goal to teach. Most of us make it our goal to control them. There's a basic law of learning that states we can't teach someone we're trying to control.

The call to compliance is designed to get kids to move back onto the pathway of God's truth, even if they don't want to. Trying to force kids to live our way is not teaching them. It's not helping them think. It's not giving them the information they need in order to decide what kind of persons they want to be—persons who live outside God's circle of truth or ones who live inside it.

This is a tragedy, because most kids end up making this decision without much data or input from their parents.

I've been with kids before at youth groups and tried an experiment that proves this point. I've stood in front of a group of Christian teenagers and said:

"Let's talk about sex."

"I want you to help me write down on the chalkboard all the biblical reasons for not being sexually active until you're married."

Nothing.

After a long pause with no response, "OK. You call them out and I'll write them down."

Silence.

"Go ahead." But the kids just sat there. So I asked them why they had no response.

"We don't know any biblical reasons why we shouldn't have sex."

"OK, let's make this easy. I'll just write down all the reasons your parents have given you why you shouldn't be sexually active before marriage. Just call them out and I'll write them down."

Still nothing! No response. Just silence.

So I said, "What's wrong?"

"Well, our parents haven't given us reasons. They just say: 'Don't.' "

"You mean you have to make the decision about whether you're going to be the kind of person that's sexually active or not, without any data? I mean there's at least twenty-seven reasons in the Scripture why you shouldn't be sexually active before marriage, and no one's given you that data?"

Doesn't it seem funny that, though God has given us a book of data, instead of using it to teach our kids so that they can make life's most important decisions, we hide the data from them and try to control their behavior. Given the opportunity to teach, we try to manipulate.

That's the opposite of what God wants. God doesn't want robots being controlled from the outside—externally. He wants people who are controlled inwardly, by the truth. How are we going to help our teens be controlled by the truth unless we teach it to them?

If we give them biblical information—information modeled for them in our lives—many more kids will voluntarily choose to live inside the circle of truth.

Kids are not stupid. Many of them, given the full truth, will desire to be the kind of people God wants them to be. There's so much to teach them at this age. We could have so much fun talking with our kids, dialoguing with them, getting down and grappling with the issues!

The alternative to teaching is to get into an arm wrestling match with them, trying to get them to comply.

Consider the consequences of this. Excitement is missing from the lives of those of us who call our kids to compliance. There's a distance between us and our kids. The distance increases the more we try to control them. We want to get away from them because of the constant conflict. They want to get away from us. That's why our kids associate God with bad feelings about themselves. When we mention Him, they feel put down, condemned, written off. Their repulsion to the truth increases. Their deception also increases. They become professional fakes. They pretend to live in conformity with God's standards just to avoid hassles, but live a different lifestyle when we aren't around—double lives.

It's certain kids will wander off the track of truth from time to time. When they do, parents will send out a call.

Ever hear parents calling their young children in the supermarket?

"Get over here! I said don't pick that up!" We hear this and wonder what it's going to be like for this parent when his or her kids become teenagers. How will such parents be talking to their kids then? They are already practicing their call. By the time their kids get to be teenagers they'll really be in a rut. Everything they say will have the same ring to it.

How do we avoid or get out of this rut? How do we develop a more effective call? We need to take Jesus' counsel when He told the Pharisees to go and learn what it means to desire compassion, not compliance.

Old Testament message: compliance doesn't work

Where can we go to learn this? For an answer, let's go to the Old Testament book of Hosea, which Jesus quoted to the Pharisees.

The nation of Israel had moved off the pathway of God's truth. In this book, God tries to persuade them to move back to the right way. In Hosea 6:1–3, it seems like Israel has already moved back on the path:

> Come let us return to the LORD.
> He has torn us to pieces,
>   but he will heal us;
> he has injured us
>   but he will bind up our wounds.
> After two days he will revive us;
>   on the third day he will restore us,
>   that we may live in his presence.
> Let us acknowledge the LORD;
>   let us press on to acknowledge him.
> As surely as the sun rises,
>   he will appear;
> he will come to us like the winter rains,
>   like the spring rains that water the earth.

Sounds like they're moving back, like they're coming around, doesn't it? But there's something still missing. The whole point of the Old Testament is to show that forcing people to comply will not cause them to move onto God's pathway and continue there.

God brought a lot of disastrous consequences on these folks because of their rebellion. Just to escape these, they've decided to comply: We don't want these disastrous consequences. We don't want these other nations coming and conquering us. We don't want our crops going bad. We don't want these plagues. Let's move back onto God's pathway of truth. Then we won't have all these bad things happening to us.

But compliance isn't what God was after. He had a different goal. He answers them, in verses 4–6,

> What can I do with you, Ephraim?
>> What can I do with you Judah?
> Your love is like the morning mist,
>> like the early dew that disappears.
> Therefore I cut you in pieces with my prophets,
>> I killed you with the words of my mouth;
>> my judgments flashed like lightning
> upon you.
> For I desire mercy, not sacrifice,
>> and acknowledgment of God
>> rather than burnt offerings.

Although the people of Israel outwardly complied, they still lacked voluntary love. He wanted them to love Him voluntarily. This was His goal!

What's our goal?

Our goal as parents determines which approach we use. What is our ultimate goal as we approach our kids?

Is our goal just to get our kids through college and married so that we can retire and live happily ever after? If that's it, guess what approach we're going to be using? Compliance. Our goal determines our approach.

God says His goal is not just to get people living happily ever after. His goal isn't just to get people conforming to Him behaviorally: offering their sacrifices, regularly coming to church, showing up on time, then going home, and being pretty good people. That's not His goal. Nor should it be ours, for it would be calling our kids to behavioral conformity.

God is after so much more than that. His goal is to have our kids' hearts with Him. He wants the kind of affection from our kids that we want from our spouses. He wants the kind of loyalty from our kids that we want from our closest friends. He wants the kind of intimate relationship with our kids that we've dreamed of, that we've wished for all our lives.

That's what God wants. And that's what He wants as our parenting goal—to get our kids together with Him in an intimate relationship.

So when a problem erupts (I can't believe our kid is cheating at school!) before we respond, we stop and think, What's my goal? Is my goal just to cut out his cheating so I don't get any more of these stupid letters from school and feel embarrassed? Or am I thinking, How am I going to get this kid to move his heart next to God's?

God says, "I desire mercy," I desire people to know Me. That's my kid's problem, he doesn't really know the Lord. His heart is not really next to Him. That's what I desire.

Perhaps we can begin to look at problems differently. As we approach them, our goal will be something more than just finding a way to live happily ever after. Our goal can be a deep, intimate relationship between God and our kids. Even though we may have no idea how to accomplish that on our own, it can still be our goal. When we teach or approach our kids, it will be the uppermost thing in our minds. How are we going to get their hearts together with God's heart? We need to call our teenagers to compassion. We need to call them to bring their hearts close to God's heart.

Remember, though, we can never call our sons and daughters to a place we haven't reached ourselves. In an earthquake, if I'm standing in one corner, I can't convince everyone else in the room to go stand in another corner. They wouldn't trust me.

If we're going to call our children to move their hearts next to God's, guess where our hearts have to be? Right next to Him, too. That's what God is after.

Three

Satisfying Our Hungry Hearts

Judy wants to die. At least, that's what she wrote in a poem for a class at school, causing school officials to spring into action. Her parents, Fred and Myrna, were asked by the school counselors to come in for a meeting to discuss the poem.

"Yes," said Judy, "I often want to take my life."

Now, that's a problem. Judy is definitely off the pathway of truth. But where should her parents start as they try to solve the problem? Where do her suicidal feelings come from?

Perhaps they come from the fact that this girl is almost forty-five pounds overweight for her height. "Helping" her lose this weight has become a family preoccupation.

Or maybe the desire to kill herself springs from a traumatic experience as a child. She was molested by a teenage boy who was her baby-sitter.

A third possibility exists. All her life she has been pitted in competition with her older brother. He went to the same school, was a straight-A student, student body president, and top athlete. As a result, Judy is known as "Randy's sister." She is under a lot of pressure to live up to Randy's achievements.

Any or all of these problems could be fueling the suicidal feelings. Every area of her life seems affected. She lost three part-time jobs. Her health isn't good. Her relationships with her friends at school are deteriorating. Her grades took a major fall. She is in a nose dive.

So what do Judy's parents do next? They've hospitalized her. They've put her on medication. They've gotten her into counseling. They've tried everything. Now they are desperate.

Desperate parents tend to parent from a position of pressure instead of from a position of rest. Fred and Myrna have tried to call Judy onto the path of truth by using anything they could to control her behavior. Compliance, not compassion, was their goal.

Judy, however, isn't the only one feeling pressured. Fred and Myrna put a lot of pressure on themselves as well. Imagine the stress they feel. "If we can't figure out a way tonight to control this girl's behavior, she might be dead tomorrow."

What are they to do? Where do they go from here? How can they rest while parenting a daughter like Judy?

Brothers fight over inheritance

Let's look to the Bible again for an answer to these crucial questions. In the book of Luke, chapter 12, Jesus had a counseling session with one person who was operating out of pressure.

Verse 13 records, as Jesus was moving through a crowd, someone said to Him, "Teacher, tell my brother to divide the inheritance with me."

Jesus gave a startling response: "Who appointed me a judge or an arbiter between you?" (v. 14). Another way to say this is, Who appointed me to referee between you?

Ever get appointed unwillingly as a referee between two people? Sometimes when my kids start fighting one of them appeals to me. "Dad, she said, I'm a jerk. Are you going to let her say that to me?" All of a sudden I've been appointed my kids' referee.

That's what happened here. Two brothers couldn't get along and one brother came and asked Jesus to make his brother share the inheritance with him. Jesus' response was revealing. He didn't allow Himself to get pulled into a role He didn't want to play. The man asked, Lord, there's someone in my life who's not giving me what I deserve. Will you make him give me what I deserve?

Notice how similar that is to the concerns we bring to God about our kids:

> Lord, my daughter isn't cooperating with me. Will You make her cooperate with me?
>
> Lord, will You make my son respect me?
>
> Now all I ask, Lord, is a little appreciation from these kids.
>
> God, I've done so much for them why won't they appreciate me?
>
> Our son is not keeping our rules. Tell him he ought to keep our rules.
>
> Lord, do something to my daughter's head that will shape her up. Give her a pill, some magic potion . . . anything!

These requests come out of pressure. Do you hear the pressure behind them? We want our kids to cooperate; we want our kids to change their behavior. Notice how Jesus responds to this kind of request. He said to the man, "Watch out!"

Why did He say that? Could it be the man was looking in the wrong place? He's looking one way; Jesus wants him to look another. Jesus said, You're not paying attention to the right things. What you really ought to be on guard against is your own greed, not your brother's. What you really need to watch is your own life, not someone else's.

Then Jesus launched into a parable about a certain rich man and his harvest. By now the man who had asked the question was probably thinking, Come on, Jesus we're talking about my brother. We're not talking about farming, OK? We're talking about my brother not sharing his inheritance.

But the Lord was thinking, Hold on. The lesson in this parable is the lesson you need to hear. Luke 12:16–21 recounts the parable Jesus told:

> The ground of a certain rich man produced a good crop. He thought to himself, "What shall I do? I have no place to store my crops." Then he said, "This is what I'll do. I will tear down my barns and build bigger ones, and there I will store all my grain and my goods. And I'll say to myself, 'You have plenty of good things laid up for many years. Take life easy; eat, drink and be merry.' " But God said to him, "You fool! This very night your life will be demanded from you. Then who will get what you have prepared for yourself?"
>
> This is how it will be with anyone who stores up things for himself but is not rich toward God.

Notice the rich man's motto: life consists in the abundance of my possessions. This is the very philosophy the brother was applying to his relationships. And if we're not careful, it's the philosophy we carry into our parenting. This philosophy, which Jesus called greed, whispers ideas like these: If I could just get more attention from others, if I could just get more respect, more appreciation, more money, then, I could rest and enjoy life.

Jesus warned us to watch out for this philosophy. The word *greed* hits us like cold water. And Jesus' advice—at first—seems impractical, irrelevant, beside the point. We're confused and reply, Jesus, I've got a daughter who's considering committing suicide and You're telling me to guard against all kinds of greed. What's greedy about wanting my kid to live?

Actually, "greed" is very similar in meaning to the word *hunger*. Jesus said to be on guard against all kinds of appetites—all kinds of hungers. Don't let your own needs dictate your responses to others.

To help our teens, we must look at our hungry hearts

If we approach the problems we're having with our teens with hunger in our own hearts, we're not going to be in the position to help them or to solve the problems. In fact, the chances are that anything we do will be fundamentally wrong. We're going to go off in the wrong direction. So we might take Jesus' teaching here and state it in a principle of parenting: When we're faced with problems with our kids, we must start with our own hungry hearts.

If I approach my kids with a hungry, restless heart, like the wronged brother or the rich farmer, I will be too consumed with my own needs to see my kids' needs clearly. A parent with a hungry heart wants more from his or her kids:

I've got to have more help from you kids.

Don't you understand that I am real preoccupied at work and I need your help when I come home?

You need to get a job. We need help on the bills.

I need more from you kids, do you understand me?

Could I get a little cooperation around here?

Jesus, in essence, warned us to be on guard against using our relationships to satisfy our hungry hearts. Every parent should guard against this in our relationships with our teens. Ecclesiastes 6:7 says, "All man's efforts are for his mouth, yet his appetite is never satisfied." In the context of the Old Testament, the author is not talking about a physical mouth and a physical stomach. He's talking about a spiritual type of appetite. All too often our efforts of building good relationships are aimed at satisfying our own appetites. But these kinds of appetites can never be satisfied in this way.

That's why Jesus chose the word *greed*, because greed is that fundamental human belief that says life depends on getting more out of others than I'm getting.

We want our kids to satisfy our hungry hearts

The hungry heart cries out and says I've got to have more than I've got today. As I approach my teenage children with a hungry heart, they can't possibly satisfy it for long. Consider why we decided to have children in the first place. Many of us thought, We want to have kids because it will be rewarding, because it will be satisfying.

What were we saying?—possibly our hearts hunger for something that we think bearing children will give us. We want to hold some little bundle of life in our arms and have this little bundle of life totally depend on us and have its little eyes look into our eyes and say, You are like a god to me. If we could have that, our hearts would finally be satisfied, right?

Teens give our hungry hearts heartburn

Yes, but it's only temporary. The older the kids get the harder it is for them to satisfy our hungry hearts. When they get into adolescence, not only do they not satisfy our hungry hearts, they inflame them. They give us heartburn.

Why is that? Why do teenagers tend to aggravate whatever problems might already be going on in our hearts? We could probably think of dozens of reasons. Let's concentrate on three.

In our society our worth is often measured by the product of our parenting. That's why we put so much pressure on our kids to get good grades, to get into good colleges, to get good occupations, to marry well.

Too often our worth seems to be riding on our children's success. In past generations the worth of a family was measured by its ancestors. A family looked to its patriarchs, grandfathers, and grandmothers to demonstrate its character.

Today's society looks to the future. All the hopes of our families are riding on the new generation. We fear our whole family's reputation will be destroyed if our kids don't make it.

A second reason our hungry hearts are inflamed is that *our children's teen years usually occur when we, the adults, are the most in need of some kind of reassurance of self-worth.*

The first decade in our careers is behind us. We've discovered by now that we probably aren't going to make company president. We've decided we're probably not going to be a six-figure-income family. We've given up on the Porsches, the yachts, etc. Many of our dreams aren't going to be realized. We're sort of on hold and we're wondering if we're worth anything any more.

In the midst of this—here come our children's teenage years. Every day we go out and fight for our self-worth on the job. Then we come home to our families, hoping for a little reassurance.

It's a period of time when our marriages are going through the doldrums. We've been married now for thirteen, fourteen, fifteen years, or more. Some marriages don't make it through this period. It's a tough time, when often we're functioning only on the basis of commitment. We don't feel the romance, and we wonder if we're still desirable.

This is also a time when we're changing physically. Our metabolism has begun to change. We don't have the energy we had, nor the physical attractiveness. We can't turn to our parents as before. They are getting up in years. They're slowing down. They're depending more on us.

We're feeling pressure from our marriages, pressure from our parents, pressure from our careers, pressure from the church and other groups who look to us for leadership. There's pressure everywhere.

So we turn to our pride and joy—our teenagers. We look into their eyes, and guess what we see? Disgust. That doesn't help our hearts rest. It only inflames them.

There's a third reason why our teenagers inflame our hearts instead of putting them at rest. *Our emotional bonds with our kids are getting stretched.*

Most parents have developed an emotional attachment with their kids before the children enter adolescence. What do you think happens to that emotional bond now?

Remember, the most important task our kids have to accomplish during adolescence is to decide what kind of persons they want to be. In order to accomplish that task they have to pull away from us for a short period of time.

With some kids it's only for a few months. With others, it can be years. They have to break—or at least stretch—the emotional bonds in order to make independent decisions. Only after they've decided what kind of persons they're going to be can they move back into relationship with us and enjoy being around us.

This separation is taking place at a time when we are hungry emotionally. We're used to having this close parent/child relationship. We relished those heart-to-hearts with our kids. We cherished the opportunities to hold them on our laps and read books to them. We enjoyed this emotionally warm, nourishing relationship. Now they're teenagers; they pull away from us. Our hearts ache.

The empty ball field

This is how Sam felt. One day as he was driving down the road, he noticed a ball diamond, and his eyes began to fill with tears. He said to himself, This is silly. Why am I feeling this way just looking at a ball diamond? Then he flashed back to the days when he watched his sons play Little League. He remembered coaching them and cheering for them.

"I'll never have those experiences with my boys again," he muttered to himself. That was such a heart-warming experience for him to have his boys in Little League and to share it all with them.

"Now that's gone. It will never happen again. Now I'm lucky if I even get a grunt from them when I walk in the door."

Consequences of not dealing with our hungry hearts

There's no question if we haven't dealt with our hungry hearts by the time our kids get to adolescence the consequences will be serious.

We'll experience distorted judgment.

The man who approached Jesus about his brother had a hungry heart that had been inflamed by not getting his inheritance. Jewish law set down rules to decide the matter, but this man was acting like a major injustice had been committed. His judgment had become distorted. An inflamed heart has a tendency to take small problems and magnify them. A hungry heart loses perspective and makes problems with others seem more serious than they really are.

The worst time to go grocery shopping is when we're hungry. The worst time to make decisions about our kids' problems is when our hearts are inflamed. If we're hungering simply for peace and quiet, what kind of parents are we going to be? Are we going to make wise decisions when our needs are at odds with our kids' needs? I once overheard a father say to his daughter, "Go ahead and date whoever you want. Just don't tell your mother, OK? I don't want to come home and have to deal with her hysteria." This father was more concerned with satisfying his own need for peace and quiet than he was with loving his daughter.

We'll experience distorted relationships.

Here's a man who came to Jesus and said, Make my brother do this. He displayed little regard for what the brother was thinking or feeling. He was saying: It will be in my best interest for you, Lord, to do a better job of controlling my brother. When we approach others with hungry hearts our relationships start to feel a lot like bad investments. We feel cheated, especially by the people closest to us.

Wait a minute! When I signed on to be a parent, I was supposed to get something out of it. I'm not getting what I thought I would.

When we said our marriage vows I remember you promised a lot of stuff to me and I'm not getting that stuff.

This seems like a bad investment. I'm not sure I should have ever gotten into parenting or marriage.

Look, we had a deal. I provide your room, board, tuition, and give you everything a child needs. In return you're supposed to admire me, appreciate me, and make me look really good around my friends. Now it's turning out to be a bad investment. I put out all this money up front, and I'm not getting back what I'm supposed to.

When our hearts become occupied with these kinds of thoughts the people around us get treated like things. Our relationships with them become distorted. We leave them feeling like pieces of furniture that we're trying to rearrange to suit our needs.

We'll experience a distorted picture of God.

The man who came to Jesus about his inheritance had a distorted picture of God. He was saying to Jesus, Hey, if you're the referee around here, how come you're not making better calls? I'm not getting my hungry heart satisfied. Come on, blow a whistle on my brother. Blow a whistle.

Jesus, however, refused to be a referee. In so many words He said, I'm not going to be the distorted God you want me to be. That's not who I am.

When we allow our hungry hearts to distort our judgment and our relationships, our picture of God is next. We become so angry at this "lousy referee" who isn't making the right calls.

When we approach our teenagers with hungry hearts, the consequences are destructive: distorted judgment, distorted relationships, and a distorted picture of God, all of which cripple us and set us up to make disastrous mistakes parenting our kids.

The surgeon discovers his family

Take Alex—a brilliant surgeon and the father of four teenagers. He experienced something that often happens with men in mid-life when they start to get into the period of time we call career stagnation (anywhere from our mid-30's to our mid-40's). Suddenly, they realize that they've invested 99 percent of their emotional energy in something that is not paying off. Their careers don't really satisfy their hungry hearts. Disillusioned, they get to a point where they want to invest all this emotional energy somewhere else.

Usually they turn to their families. At this point, thoughts like this went through Alex's mind: Hey, I've been away from my family a lot. I've spent years in that hospital. But you know, I have a hunger that just can't be satisfied at the hospital, so I'm going to give my family an opportunity to satisfy my hungry heart. Family—that's where it's at! I've been such a fool for ignoring my family. I'm going to make it up to them. I'm going to buy all these expensive toys for us and we're going to have great family times.

That's what this brilliant man decided. But Alex forgot that he was a stranger to his family. His kids didn't know him. His wife didn't know him.

All of a sudden he started hanging around the house, coming up with all these family activities. He wanted his family's time, attention, and affection. This man with a hungry heart was all over his wife and kids with demands.

They didn't know what to do with him. They'd long since replaced Dad with the television. (A national survey a few years back asked kids whether they preferred Dad or television. Most chose television. Because they know television, their best friends are on that TV set. Their dad—they don't know him.)

So, as Alex moved toward his family with his hungry heart, he found them unresponsive; they didn't want him around. He impulsively bought a camper and thousands of dollars worth of fishing equipment so they could enjoy the great outdoors together; they didn't like camping. All they wanted to do was sit home and watch movies on the VCR.

And so Alex came into the church and demanded that we as a church take more of a stand on television. He literally shouted, "THE PROBLEM WITH OUR COUNTRY AND THE PROBLEM WITH OUR FAMILIES IS THAT PEOPLE HAVEN'T BEEN TAUGHT ABOUT THE DESTRUCTIVE-NESS OF TELEVISION!"

What's going on with Alex? His heart was so hungry that his judgment was distorted. He came to the conclusion that the real problem with his family is television. Know what the Lord would say to Alex?

Watch out for your hungry heart. It was your own hunger that took you away from your family. You ignored them for years because you were getting your hunger satisfied at work. Now you demand that your family satisfy it.

No wonder Paul warned his readers, "If you keep on biting and devouring each other, watch out or you will be destroyed by each other" (Gal. 5:15).

Three sentences from Jesus

So what's a parent like Alex, with a hungry heart, to do?

Listen to three sentences from Luke 12 that Jesus spoke in response to the wronged brother. In them He gives us three keys for dealing with our hungry hearts.

Be on your guard against all kinds of greed (v. 15).

There are all kinds of passions and appetites stirring in our hearts that will head us off in the wrong directions with our kids.

If we're going to be on guard against this, maybe the best question to ask ourselves is what kind of hunger drives us the most? What kind of hunger poses the greatest obstacle to our being effective parents? Maybe I'm a single parent who has a deep sense of loneliness. I need to be on guard for how that loneliness, that deep hunger to be wanted by somebody, affects my parenting.

Whenever I am faced with a decision that could be unpopular with my daughter, I don't want to make it on the basis of my hungry heart, which cries out to be cherished by somebody.

Identifying what we hunger for the most helps us to be on guard that it doesn't distort the way we parent.

What are you hungry for right now? Can you put it into words? This is what my heart is aching for. This is what my tongue is hanging out for. This is it.

We can't be on guard against something unless we first put a finger on it.

A person's life does not consist in the abundance of his possessions (v.15).

If you're sitting at home on the couch watching TV and all of a sudden your stomach growls, you realize, I'm hungry. What will you do? Reach for the first thing that will quiet that hunger, right? Jesus warned, "Watch out!" When you're heart is hungry, don't impulsively reach for some thing or some person to quiet your hunger. You can't use someone to satisfy your hungry heart and love that person at the same time. The two cancel each other out. He said, Don't give in to the idea your lives depend on how much you can get of a certain item from other people."

Suicide at college

Sue and Frank were parents who put extreme pressure on their teenage daughters. These girls were valedictorian types. They had the top grades. They always looked like a million dollars. They were involved in all the right things in church. They made their parents proud. To outsiders, Sue and Frank looked so together, like the ideal Christian parents—so stable and mature.

In college, one of their girls started to get some low grades and, without warning, committed suicide. Over night, Sue and Frank's world fell apart.

For years, their hungry hearts were being satisfied through their daughters' achievements. The kids felt so much pressure because they thought Mom and Dad's happiness depended on them.

No one could understand why their oldest daughter

couldn't live with the possibility of getting an F in a class. No one knew the incredible pressure she lived under.

As soon as the illusion of the perfect family was shattered, it became obvious that Sue and Frank were very needy. Everything started coming apart. They screamed at each other constantly. They talked openly about separation and divorce. Their other daughter became suicidal.

The moral: we can look pretty healthy and mature as long as our kids cooperate and satisfy our hungry hearts. But the difficult events of life make it impossible for us to use them this way for very long.

Jesus' first sentence said we should pay attention to our own hungry hearts. His second sentence said we shouldn't give in to the temptation to use people or things to quiet our hunger. The Lord's third sentence tells us how we can put our hungry hearts into a position of rest.

Learn to be rich toward God (v. 21).

Is there anything about that sentence that strikes you as ironic? A man who thought he didn't have enough money is told to be rich toward God. What can we possibly give to make God richer? All we have to offer Him is ourselves, with our hungry hearts.

That's hard for us when we are preoccupied with getting nourishment for ourselves. How do we give our hearts to God instead of nourishing ourselves with substitutes? The answer is in Revelation, chapter 3, verses 17–19:

> You say, "I am rich; I have acquired wealth and do not need a thing." But you do not realize you are wretched, pitiful, poor, blind and naked. I counsel you to buy from me gold refined in the fire, so you can become rich; and white clothes to wear, so you can cover your shameful nakedness, and salve to put on your eyes, so you can see.

Those whom I love I rebuke and discipline. So be earnest, and repent. Here I am! I stand at the door and knock. If anyone hears my voice and opens the door, I will come in and eat with him, and he with me.

Jesus was speaking to a group of believers in the ancient city of Laodicea, but His description of them as wretched, pitiful, poor, blind, and naked, has a very modern application for parents. There are very few things that are more effective at exposing us as the wretched, pitiful, poor, blind and naked people we truly are than our own adolescent children. All the illusions we have about ourselves pop like balloons. Jesus was saying, You say you have your act all together. You don't need anything. Let me tell you folks, you need so much. You're a mess. For a fact, you're wretched, pitiful, poor, blind, and naked.

We're a hungry bunch of parents

Jesus' counsel is to get what will satisfy our hungry and impoverished condition from Him, and Him alone. Admit how hungry you are. Quit pretending that you have it all together. Go to Him and say, "I'm so cotton-pickin' hungry. I've looked all week for one compliment. I am just so hungry for someone to notice what I'm doing. I am so hungry, Lord, for someone to want to be near me. I am so hungry for someone to pat me on the back and say, man, you're really good!

What do you hunger for? Put it into words. Whatever you identify you can use to approach God. He delights in meeting our needs.

This was the first step Fred and Myrna took to help Judy, their overweight, suicidal daughter. They said, "God, we don't have our act together. We don't know what we're doing with our kids. We're confused. Our family has all kinds of problems. Our daughter is writing poems at school about committing suicide. We don't know what to do with her, God. We're so hungry for things to go right for her. We bring our hungry hearts to you. We invite your Son, Jesus Christ, into our hungry hearts. He promised if we opened the door to Him, He will come in and eat with us."

Intimate dinners with God

The only remedy for a hungry heart is to have intimate dinners with God's Son. When was the last time you sat and had an intimate dinner with the Lord? When was the last time you chewed on things together with Him?

That's the only thing that really satisfies the hungering human heart—an intimate relationship with Jesus Christ. Without it there's no rest. We're going to be in that frantic position of pressure.

Before we can effectively parent, our hearts must be at rest. It's so sad that many of us are running around trying to use everything else to satisfy our hungry hearts when the Lord Jesus Christ is waiting for us to come to Him. He's right there knocking on your heart's door wanting to dine with you.

What comes into your mind when I talk about having intimate dinners with the Lord Jesus Christ?

Think about packing a sack lunch and going out somewhere to meet the Lord for an intimate chat. Just the two of you—you give yourself to Him, and He'll nourish you.

How about inviting Him for a drive, or a walk, or bicycling, or even jogging?—Will You hold my hand and come along with me? Be with me. Right now, God, there's not a person in the world I feel loves or respects me. Will You come and walk along with me?

These are the kinds of intimate conversations with the Lord Jesus Christ we need. Without them, it is impossible to approach our kids with our hearts at rest. It's not about just telling Him what we need; it's about making time to let Him personally meet those needs.

Four

Finding the Ultimate Solution

When problems hit teenagers, parents often think the solution lies in changing the friends their kids hang out with. Ever tried it? That's often behind parents moving their kids from school to school—to get them away from bad influences, friends who are pulling them down.

This was the case with Cindy and her family. Cindy was in a lot of trouble. She was arrested for shoplifting. Shortly after that she appeared to be drunk at school, so officials searched her locker and found alcohol. She began cutting school frequently.

Her parents assumed that it was her friends who were pressuring her to behave this way. So they withdrew her from public school and moved her to a Christian school.

New friends, new attitude

Happily, the problem behavior stopped. Cindy didn't seem to be drinking anymore. She showed up on time for her classes and never skipped school. She wasn't stealing anymore, either. She seemed to settle down. The rest of her high school years saw no more episodes of defiant behavior.

But when she went to college, something happened. Just a few weeks into the first semester Cindy started skipping classes and drinking heavily at the various sorority open houses. She was caught cheating on an English assignment.

The problem behaviors were back. So were her parents' fears and questions.

"Where did we go wrong with Cindy? We thought we solved this problem by getting her away from bad influences in high school. We can't keep doing that the rest of her life."

A lot of us are like Cindy's parents. We grasp something that seems to work when our teen first has problems, only to see the problem surface a few months or a few years later. What seemed to be the ultimate solution turned out to be only temporary.

Temporary solutions waste our time

A lot of techniques will temporarily change teenagers. We can usually get them to comply behaviorally with either the threat of pain or the promise of pleasure. When those don't work, a change of environment—new school, new friends, new church—may.

However, external pressure or changes of environment are never the ultimate solution to our kids' problems. This only leads them to get back on the path and comply as long as we keep up the pressure or we control their environment.

When the pressure stops, our teens move right back off the path because nothing inside them has changed. They are not personally committed to live on the track of truth. They stay there only because of external factors.

The ultimate solution requires our teens to make a change of heart. It requires something inside them to change, causing them to want to live on the path of truth no matter what's going on around them. But how in the world do we accomplish this? We have trouble getting them to pick up their dirty underwear without being asked—let alone getting them to obey God on their own!

How do we help them move from point A—complying only when they have to—to what seems like point Z—where they're actually living for God because they want to? What's the ultimate solution to that? Knowing the ultimate solution is the most important part of formulating a game plan for parenting.

There's not a basketball team that brings the ball inbounds and starts the game without knowing where the basket is. It may be a hundred yards down the court; it's a long way to go, and it may seem like we'll never get down there, but it's important that we begin the game knowing where the goal is.

What is the ultimate solution? If we don't include it in our game plan, we will fall into using temporary solutions. To understand this, let's once again turn to the Bible, to Ephesians 2:1–6:

> As for you, you were dead in your transgressions and sins, in which you used to live when you followed the ways of this world and of the ruler of the kingdom of the air, the spirit who is now at work in those who are disobedient. All of us also lived among them at one time, gratifying the cravings of our sinful natures and following its desires and thoughts. Like the rest, we were by nature objects of wrath. But because of his great love for us, God, who is rich in mercy, made us alive with Christ even when we were dead in transgressions—it is by grace you have been saved. And God raised us up with Christ and seated us with him in the heavenly realms in Christ Jesus.

Notice the forces the Bible says are at work to get people to live outside God's moral boundaries: internal ones, like "the cravings of our sinful nature," as well as external ones, like "the ways of the world"—incredible forces! Both pressure our kids to get off the track of truth.

What is God's solution? He makes us alive with Christ. He raises us with Christ and seats us with Him in the heavenly realms. In fact, one of the names of Christ when He came on the first Christmas was *Emmanuel*, which means, "God with us." "Witness" is an important concept in the Bible.

The ultimate solution: hanging out with God

Cindy's parents were right when they assumed that the friends Cindy hung out with were important. However, the ultimate solution, the key to seeing her grow into the kind of person who wants to live in the track of God's truth, was not getting her to hang out with the right people. It was getting her to hang out with Christ.

These two words, "with Christ," represent the ultimate solution for every problem that plagues our kids. Getting our kids together with Christ should always be the goal of Christian parenting.

Teenagers like to hang out. Often they'll hang out with non-Christian kids. Sometimes they'll hang out with Christian kids. Other times they'll hang out with adults who are working with their youth group.

Only one person, though, with whom they can hang out has the power to change them from the inside out and to give them a heart of compassion; only He can make them want to live within God's moral boundaries, walking the path of truth. There's only one person.

When I was newly a youth pastor, I foolishly tried to portray to parents that I had this kind of power. "Listen, do you have a problem with your kids? Send them to me. Just spending time with me every week for a few hours—just being in my presence—will be like radiation treatments. There's something about my presence that's going to purify and cleanse them from the inside out. If you'll give them to me for a few years, they'll be different people."

I discovered that no matter how much time I spent with a kid, no matter what techniques I used, I didn't have the power to change the type of person she was on the inside. And so it is with any parent, youth worker, or counselor. We're just human beings.

But Jesus Christ is unlike any mere human being. Yes, He's human. But He's God, as well. Being in His presence is like having the strongest radiation treatment that exists. But it's not a radiation treatment that kills physical cancer cells; it's a radiation treatment that kills spiritual cancer cells.

By hanging out with Jesus Christ—being in His presence, talking with Him—a transformation of the heart occurs. There's something about His presence that purifies and cleanses. It's impossible to be with Him for very long without deep changes occurring. Read the pages of the Gospels for ample proof of this.

The ultimate solution to our kids' problems is a deeper, more real, personal, intimate relationship with Jesus Christ. Christian parents should occupy themselves with the thought, How can I encourage my teen to hang out with Christ, just as she would with a close, merely human, friend.

That's the ultimate solution.

Hanging out with Christ is a reachable goal

It might seem like an unachievable goal. Between us and our goal, the basket, is the world's biggest, best team, one that has never been defeated. The situation seems impossible. But now we know where the goal is. We know where we need to go.

If we can somehow move our kids to the place where they're hanging out with Jesus Christ the change of heart we want to see will occur. That's our goal.

As a youth worker, I dealt with hundreds of parents. However, seldom did any of them come to me and say, "I'm wondering what can I do to motivate my teenager to want to be with Jesus. Do you have any ideas on how we can get the two of them together?"

Why is it that so few of us spend time thinking about Christ as the ultimate solution?

Could it be that we—even Christian parents—believe the ultimate solution really lies somewhere else? Let's look at another counseling session, this time between Jesus and a woman who was making this very mistake.

> As Jesus and his disciples were on their way, he came to a village where a woman named Martha opened her home to him. She had a sister called Mary, who sat at the Lord's feet listening to what he said. But Martha was distracted by all the preparations that had to be made. She came to him and asked, "Lord, don't you care that my sister has left me to do the work by myself? Tell her to help me!"
>
> "Martha, Martha," the Lord answered, "you are worried and upset about many things, but only one thing is needed. Mary has chosen what is better, and it will not be taken away from her" (Luke 10:38–42).

Here's an older sister who wanted the exact opposite of what we've been talking about for her younger sister. Mary wanted to hang out with Jesus. But her sister Martha wanted her to do something else instead—something Martha considered much more important. Remember, the older sister was a follower of Jesus herself. However, even she lost sight of the goal.

What's going on here with Martha may very well be the same thing that's often going on with parents.

It's important to observe how the Lord answers her: "Martha, Martha, you are worried and upset about many things, but only one thing is needed." Only one thing is crucial or essential to your existence, and Mary has chosen that. "It will not be taken away from her."

Martha's irresponsible little sister

When she came to Jesus, Martha was probably putting her finger on a real problem. This may not have been the first time Mary abandoned Martha in the kitchen. Usually we don't get upset over one-time incidents, right? We get upset when we see a pattern of irresponsibility developing in our kids. It irks us. Martha is probably irked because Mary's actions are part of a whole pattern. She's thinking, Mary always does this! She's always leaving me this way. So Martha came to Jesus and complained, Are you going to let Mary get away with her irresponsibility?

A parent says to the Lord, Are you going to let my teenager get away with her disrespect? Lord, tell her to obey me. Tell her to give me the respect that's due me as her father.

Perhaps Martha had a valid complaint. Perhaps Mary was self-centered and irresponsible at times and didn't help out enough in the kitchen. But what was Martha's solution to Mary's selfishness? Calling her to compliance. Jesus looked at things differently.

If we amplify what He said to Martha: Yes indeed, Martha, Mary does have a problem with selfishness. But you know what will solve the problem ultimately? It's not making her get into the kitchen and work. It's letting her hang out with Me. If she spends time with Me she'll learn about love from the inside out. Something will change in her heart. Then you know what will happen, Martha? Mary will want to help you out of a willing heart.

If I get on Mary's case and tell her to get in the kitchen and help you right now, that might solve the problem this time. What's going to happen the next time you're fixing dinner and I'm not here?

Our mistake: concentrating on behavior

Martha failed to aim at the ultimate solution. Jesus fixed His eyes on it: a change in Mary's heart that required spending time with Him. Martha fixed her eyes on something else: a change in Mary's behavior, and all that required was putting pressure on her. Like Martha, it's so easy for parents to get hung up on the immediate concern and forget what the ultimate solution is.

What happens when Dad comes home after buzzing around the country and finds in the mail a note from the school reporting that his daughter is failing English?—Imagine the gall of this kid! Here I am traveling, sacrificing for the family, and my daughter back at home can't even get her English assignment in on time.

How does he attempt to solve the problem? The temptation is to get mad and chew her out—shape that kid up with the threat of some painful consequences. Wonder what I could do to scare this girl into never embarrassing me with an F in English again! He looks for some way to call her to compliance—instead of looking for a way he can use this problem to bring her a step closer to the ultimate solution.

Each problem we face with our kid affords us an opportunity to move her one small step toward Christ. Although we can't move her from A to Z in one conversation, we might move her from A to B, or halfway to B. That's why it's important that parents never lose sight of the ultimate goal.

Martha lost sight of it. She attached more significance to Mary's performance level than to Mary's relationship with Christ.

Three ways of viewing behavior

When problems occur with our kids, we have to decide how much significance to attach to them.

We may decide the level of significance is only **casual**. If someone in our family is selfish and refuses to help with the dishes, we might think to ourselves: Well, it's not too big of a deal. Kids will be kids. Kids will be selfish. They all go through these phases. Good grief, I guess I ought to be thankful that she's not taking drugs! I've got the time. I'll just go do them myself. If it happens again, then we'll talk to her.

That's treating it as casual.

However, I could decide the level of significance is **serious**. This girl is really self-centered. If we don't step in here and teach her something about the consequences of selfishness, she's going to carry this into her adult life and it's going to hurt all her relationships. I'm going to enforce some consequences if she doesn't help with the dishes tonight.

This is treating it as serious.

I could, however, elevate the significance of the problem to a third level and call it **vital**. When we get to this point, we find ourselves thinking such things as: If we can't get that girl out in the kitchen to clean up the dishes our family is going to fall apart. We're all going to have nervous breakdowns. Everybody is going to be fighting and arguing. Doesn't this girl realize what's she's doing? She's going to ruin us!

See what we've done? We've raised the problem to the same level that Martha did. She magnified her sister's failure to help in the kitchen to vital importance.

Only one thing is vital

There's only one thing that's vital, and it's what Mary chose, Jesus counseled Martha. And what was that? What did Mary choose? She chose relationship with Christ.

Because relationship with Him is absolutely necessary for our well-being, Christ promised that it is the one thing that will never be taken away from us. We might lose our children. We might lose our jobs. We might lose our homes, or our spouses. But Jesus guarantees our relationship with Him will never be taken away from us.

For us and for our kids, just as for Mary, only this is vital. It's the only thing our lives really depend on. Without it, we're sunk. If we elevate anything other than relationship with Christ to this status, we commit the same sin Martha did.

Things that aren't vital

As parents, what do we elevate to this status? What things in our kid's lives do we treat as vital?

Sometimes parents treat their kids' happiness as vital. Usually we say it this way: All I want—and I'm not asking for much—is that my kids are happy. I'm not asking for anything else—just to see my kids happy.

Doesn't sound like much, does it? Not unless you're the kid. Imagine the pressure she must feel to always be up for her parents. It forces her to pretend. She always has to look happy, act happy, and make others happy. That's vital. No wonder so many kids resort to using drugs to artificially generate happiness.

Some parents treat their kids' success as vital. They might say it this way: All I ask is that my kids do their best. Now that's not too much to ask, is it? If they always do their best, they'll be a success.

Once I had a conversation with a mother who had this philosophy. I asked, "When you combed your hair this morning, did you do your best?"

"I suppose I did."

"How much time did you spend combing your hair?"

"Five or ten minutes."

"Could you have done a better job if you'd spent fifteen?"

"I suppose so."

"Well, then you blew your own principal—all you ask is that you do your best."

"Well, it's not important on things like that."

"Oh, I misunderstood. I thought you said that it was always important to do your best. Let me ask you, have you ever been asked to do projects at work?"

"Yeah."

"How many hours did you spend on the last project?"

"Maybe a hundred."

"Could you have done a better job if you'd spent a hundred and ten?"

"Oh, I suppose."

"Then you didn't do your best, did you?"

You see, doing our best is an impossible standard to reach. And if we say to our kids that their lives depend on it we're telling them that life depends on something they can't achieve.

Often parents treat our kids' achievements as vital. When a report card comes home with Ds or Fs, a conversation like this ensues:

"I don't understand why you get so upset about my grades. What's the big deal? Why is it so important that I have good grades?"

"You'll never get into a decent college if you don't have good grades."

"Why is it important that I get into a good college? I can go to community college. I know kids who even flunk out of school and they're doing OK. What's the big deal?"

"If you don't get into a decent college you won't get a decent job."

"So what if I get a job that's not paying big bucks. What's the big deal about that? I don't want to be rich."

"Well if you don't get a good salary you won't be able to have the kind of lifestyle we have. And if you don't have the kind of lifestyle that we have you won't be happy like us."

In conversations like these we're telling our kids their lives depend on their achievements, and they're not buying it. They can see in our lives how achievements aren't enough to make us happy. That's often why they hold back. They've been down that street. They've learned good grades don't produce happiness for very long.

At times we treat our kids' relationships as vital. Parents may panic when their daughter is approaching college and has never dated. They slip questions like these into their conversations with her: Don't you know any boys at school? Do you ever talk to boys? Do you always just hang out with the girls? What do you say when a boy comes up and talks to you?

What is our kid hearing when we're saying this? She hears us say that her identity and worth depend on her relationships with males. That may send her scurrying around trying to get attached to somebody—anybody!—because we've taught her she can't have a quality life without a man.

Parents even treat their kids' physical characteristics and health as vital. When we see our kid developing a physical characteristic that might bring some social rejection, it is easy to elevate it to a vital status.

More times than not, however, the physical feature then gets worse. It seldom fails that if we make a vital issue of our teenager's weight, her weight just increases. If we make a vital issue of her dress, her appearance becomes sloppier. This is her way of telling us that she resents such superficial things being treated as vital.

Most parents elevate their teen's physical well-being—safety—to a vital status. It's easy for parents to think it's our job to make sure nothing ever happens of a destructive nature to our teenagers.

Carol and Ken did this. Their daughter Heather was sexually molested when she was twelve. They decided, If this ever happens again to Heather, it will destroy her—and us—so we can't let it happen again.

They elevated her future relationships to a vital status. They put her in a protective bubble. They kept her from having dozens of normal experiences that would have helped her grow up unaffected by the molestation. The result: the girl became scarred—not only from the molestation, but from her parent's response to it.

It's easy for parents to make preventing the occurrence, or reoccurrence, of traumatic events in our kids' lives imperative. A rapist, a robber, or a mugger can cause great pain, but they can't take away our kid's capacity to be whole people. We live in a world in which even God's own suffer great harm. But whatever damage a molestation might do, it will not be vital, it will be repairable.

After a kid has been victimized, parents are wise to encourage her to resume normal activities and schedules. Although every precaution should be taken to protect the child, parents have no way of guaranteeing an event like this, or some other tragedy, will not happen again. Let your children drive, let them date, let them go off to college. Your power to keep them safe is limited. Your goal is to promote their relationship with Christ. Only this will equip them to endure and survive the trials of life. Any illusion of safety will likely be shattered by life's difficulties.

To summarize: happiness, success, achievements, friendships, health, and safety are all important areas in our teen's lives. However, at one time or another, every one of our kids will be forced to live without one or all of these. When that happens, the only thing that will be vital is their relationship with Christ. As long as that is intact, they will be OK.

Dangers of not focusing on the ultimate solution

Treating any of these things as vital to our teenager's well-being leads to serious consequences.

One consequence is that *it teaches our teenager to build her life on sand.*

Remember what Jesus said in the parable about the two men who built houses? The wise man built his house on a rock foundation, but the foolish man built his house on a foundation of sand. When the storms of life came along, the house built on sand didn't stand up (see Luke 6: 47–49).

What if we teach our kids that the quality of their lives depends upon the quality of their relationships with the opposite sex? What will happen when a spouse is taken by an accident or by divorce? Will the storm wash out the whole foundation of their lives? Not if their lives are built on a relationship with Christ.

What if we teach them that the quality of their lives depends on their standard of living? What will happen when they lose a job, a career? Many people jumped out windows when the stock market crashed in 1929. Some people commit suicide when they face financial loss.

When we teach our kids that any of these things are vital we encourage them to build their lives on something that at some point in their lives will be washed out by the storms of life.

A second consequence is that *it teaches our teenager how to make her life work—at least temporarily—apart from a relationship with Christ.*

If I believe that the quality of my daughter's life depends on keeping her happy all the time, I can keep her happy by buying her stuff. What am I doing? I'm teaching her how to make her life work without a relationship with Christ.

I'm teaching her to make spending her god, instead of Christ. This may lead to serious addictions down the road, and ultimately to bankruptcy—spiritually. I set her up for this by the way I parent her.

A third consequence is *it dilutes our parental energies so that there is very little left over for what's vital.*

Ever been so tired of dealing with kids and their problems that you don't even have the energy to pray for them? Ever been so preoccupied with what is going on in their lives that you don't have time to get alone and have a meaningful chat with the Lord?

That kind of exhaustion comes from doing what Martha did. Remember how Jesus counseled her, Martha, you're worried about so many things, your energy is flowing in so many different directions because you've made so many things vital. No wonder you don't have the time and energy to come and sit at my feet.

The same is true for parents. When faced with the option of setting aside time to sit at Jesus' feet and talk with Him about our kids, or taking on extra work so that our kids can go to one of the finest colleges, which do we choose? Which will have more impact on shaping them into the kind of people God desires? We have to be careful that we don't spend the bulk of our parental energies on that which has little or no power to shape our kids' hearts.

Kay did just that. She became pregnant while only a teenager, and gave up her baby girl for adoption. She lived with intense grief and guilt for so many years that she vowed she wouldn't let the same thing happen to any of her kids in the future.

After she married she had another daughter, Molly. As Molly approached adolescence, Kay could focus on only one thing: that her daughter never get pregnant as a teenager like she had. All her energy went in this direction. Molly grew into a beautiful girl whom the guys chased passionately.

Kay became obsessed. When Molly was in junior high, Kay would spy on her. As her daughter walked to the bus stop in the morning, she would shadow her. Out of sight, hidden by trees, Kay watched the girl to make sure she wasn't talking to boys. Sometimes this mother would get in her car and follow the school bus to watch and see who Molly talked to when she got off the bus. Kay pumped teachers for information, hoping to pick up clues for potential boy problems. Kay would listen to Molly's phone conversations. She read her daughter's diary.

She believed Molly's life would be ruined if she got pregnant in high school—even though her own life proved that this wasn't true.

Because of this belief, every ounce of her time and energy were spent trying to monitor and control the situation. Nothing was left over to invest in any other task. Soon all Kay's other relationships, with her husband, with her friends, and with the Lord, became almost nonexistent. She lost all her resources to maintain her own health and vitality, and eventually became involved in an immoral relationship herself—the very thing from which she was trying to save Molly.

A fourth consequence is that *it makes parents feel uncared for and unsupported by God.*

We feel God doesn't attach the same level of significance to our agenda that we do. We feel He doesn't care.

How did Martha feel when Jesus' agenda was not to get Mary in the kitchen? How do we feel when Jesus' agenda for our kids is not what ours is?

Don't you care? Don't you care about me, God? My daughter didn't make the beauty pageant. Don't you care? God, she didn't get straight A's. She didn't get on the cheer leading squad. She didn't get accepted in the best college. She wasn't elected president of the youth group. She didn't make the missions team. Don't you care, God?

When we raise any of these things to vital status we're surprised that God doesn't. We feel He isn't answering our prayers. He seems remote. But He is actually very involved. He says, These things aren't vital. I want to bring this girl to the point where the most important thing when she gets up in the morning is to sit at My feet. That's where I want to bring her. That's what I want to focus on.

It's all flip-flopped. What God says is vital often is the opposite of what we treat as vital.

Think of all the positive consequences of treating our kids' relationship to Christ as the only thing that is vital to their well-being.

The positives of concentrating on what is vital

I'm going to do a whole lot of talking to Jesus about my teenager and a whole lot of talking to my teenager about Jesus. Instead of a lot of talking about other things that I've mistakenly elevated to a vital status, I'm going to be talking about the only thing that is vital.

My friends don't love me!

I'll never forget facing the challenge of talking to my daughter about Christ when she was going through a period of time where she felt like nobody loved her. All her friends at school had betrayed her. She was angry, hurt.

She felt that the one vital thing in her life was her friends, and that vital thing wasn't working at the moment. To make matters worse this was also a period of time when she wasn't even sure God exists. How do you get a kid in this situation to think about her relationship with Christ?

I didn't know what to do, so I just asked her some questions. "I guess I know a little bit about what's going on with your friends at school, but I don't know a lot. I'd like to know more."

She began giving me all the details—all the hurts, disappointments, and betrayals. It took her about an hour and a half to tell them to me.

As I listened I didn't have the foggiest idea of what to say to her. I didn't want to tell her how to make her life work apart from Christ. I didn't want to agree with her that it was vital she have her friends' support, and show her how to get it.

I could have told her that. I'm pretty good at getting people to do what I want them to.

I wondered how I could move her even a baby step toward the Lord. We talked some more. I tried to feel her pain with her. Finally, I took a chance. "I know that right now you're not sure God exists. But just on the chance that He does, and that He does care about you, would it be OK with you if we talked to Him about your friends right now? I know He cares. Would you be willing to do that?"

After a long pause, she whispered, "I guess so."

So we talked to the Lord about it. I did most of the talking, although she did a little.

In the next few days, we saw God answer our prayers about her friends. In so doing, He challenged the doubt she felt whether God really exists. I asked her to pray with me again. Some more things happened with her friends over the next several weeks that were very hard to explain apart from the fact that God intervened.

She was learning two very important truths. God does exist, and her relationship with Him is far more valuable than her relationship with her friends.

Inevitably, when we get our kids talking to Jesus about the important stuff in their lives, it moves them closer to Him. It makes the stuff less important and the relationship with Him more important. It turns upside down what they deem important.

Building bridges for our kids

What can we do to move our teenagers closer to Christ? Think of it in terms of building bridges between islands for them. The first island represents the problem behaviors our kids are exhibiting. The second island is whatever is causing them to behave this way and get off the path of truth—what hunger are they trying to satisfy? Are they getting off the track because they want to be cared for? Do they want to belong? Maybe they just want to feel important. We must help them see the connection between their problems and their hunger. Whatever it might be, let's help them build this bridge in their minds.

We can be sure when our kids get off the path of truth they are hungry for something they're not getting; they don't believe satisfaction for the hunger lies on God's pathway but that they will find it another way.

As we talk to them about things they hunger for, we build another bridge, to a third island. This island is a relationship with Christ. He's the only one who can satisfy the hungers of their hearts.

Don't expect to build these bridges in one discussion. Or in one month. Bridge-building takes years. God has made adolescence so long—He's given us a lot of time to build these bridges. We're going to be talking about how we do this in upcoming chapters. It's the process called *teaching*. Teaching is nothing more than helping our kids build mental bridges.

We're going to use our kids' problems to help them see what they're hungering for and see that ultimately the only satisfaction for the hunger is Christ—having a personal relationship with Him. That's the ultimate solution!

Five

Looking for Love, Finding Rebellion

Recently, as I was driving home from work, I was feeling pretty lonely. I began wondering what I could do to feel better. I decided a walk along the beach would be just the remedy. I thought it would be perfect if my sixteen-year-old daughter would go along to keep me company.

When I arrived home I told her what I had in mind. She looked at me as if I was crazy.

"It would be good for you to get out and get some fresh air," I said.

"But it's cold and drizzling outside, Dad."

"That's OK; we'll wear raincoats."

"Well, my homework isn't done."

"There'll be plenty of time when we get back."

"But I don't want to go, Dad."

Finally I convinced her, against all her protests, to go along for her Dad's sake—just to cheer me up. As we walked along a bicycle path, she came up with several new reasons why this was an absolutely stupid idea.

"I'm tired. It's cold. My feet hurt."

It was easy to see this was not working. She was making me feel worse instead of better.

God wants voluntary love

I'd come home hoping for some voluntary love from her. Instead, all I could elicit was a little forced love. And forced love never satisfies a father's heart. God never settles for forced love, either. He wants to be loved voluntarily.

Do you remember the time that the Pharisees were criticizing Jesus for hanging out with tax collectors and sinners? Remember what He answered? "Go and learn what this means: 'I desire mercy, not sacrifice' " (Matt. 9:13). Another way of saying that is, I desire voluntary love, not forced love.

Remember how Christ answered the question, which is the most important commandment? He said, all the commandments hang on the commandments to love the Lord your God with all your heart, with all your energy, and to love your neighbor as yourself (Matt. 22:35–40). The only thing God wants from human beings is our voluntary love.

In an earlier chapter, we defined a problem as any event, relationship, or emotion that persuades our kids to get off the track of God's truth. Voluntary love is all that will keep our kids living on the pathway of God's truth over the long haul. Without it, they can never be the kind of people God desires.

Jonah—a biblical model

By now you might be asking the question, Just how does somebody come by voluntary love for God? By its very definition, this kind of love can't be anything a parent, or even God, can force on a teenager. How can such a quality be produced when it goes against our grain as selfish human beings? In the Old Testament book of Jonah we find a model that we can follow to cultivate voluntary love in the hearts of our rebellious teens. In working with rebellious Jonah, God shows us what to do. Jonah 1:1-3 says:

> The word of the LORD came to Jonah son of Amittai: "Go to the great city of Ninevah and preach against it, because its wickedness has come up before me."
>
> But Jonah ran away from the LORD and headed for Tarshish. He went down to Joppa, where he found a ship bound for that port. After paying the fare, he went aboard and sailed for Tarshish to flee from the LORD.

Notice the first step God took to cultivate love in Jonah's heart: He commanded him to love a group of people who were hard to love. The Ninevites were part of the Assyrian nation—feared and despised enemies of the Israelites.

This command came at a time Jonah was enjoying great honor in the nation of Israel. He proclaimed a very positive message. He prophesied that God was going to expand the borders of Israel. It was going to be a time of greatness (see 2 Kings 14:23–27). As a result, Jonah was a very popular prophet.

One of the most unpopular things God could have asked him to do was to preach to the Ninevites and help them escape the very judgment of God that every Israelite prayed for. Anything Jonah would do to bring a blessing on the Ninevites would be greeted by Israel as a hostile act—maybe even an act of treason.

Jonah was commanded by God to love literally his worst enemies. Why did God begin to work with Jonah's unloving heart this way? Why start with such hard people to love? Why not start with easy ones?

Are we "specialists" in love?

Today is an age of specialization. I've specialized in working with teenagers. I love being around them. They've always been easy for me to love, for some reason. Recently, however, I found myself called by God to a ministry that involved working with younger children who were very troubled. In a sense, I was forced to love them because they were a part of my job description—a job description that was rewritten after I was hired to include troubled children.

God used that experience to catapult me into a group of people difficult for me to love. He wanted me to learn a very important truth about myself—the same reason that God sent Jonah to Ninevah. Can you imagine what Jonah must have felt when he first got the invitation? No, no! Wait a minute. I specialize in loving Israelites. I'm an Israelite pastor, not a Ninevite pastor. God, why are you asking me to do this?

That's the same question I asked on the first day I did play therapy with five hyperactive nine-year-old boys: Why, God, do You ask me to love these hard-to-loves?

That's where God has to start to show us how little we know about true love. How can we even know if we love at all until we're called upon to do that which is uncomfortable for us? As long as everything we're asked to do is what we want to do anyway, how can we be sure that it's love at all? It's not until our inability to love is exposed that we'll ever be motivated to ask God to teach us how to love.

Hanging out only with the people we find easy to love doesn't expose us. However, being asked to love the less lovable exposes what's really in our hearts, shatters any illusions we might have about the kind of people we are. This is how God uses hard-to-love teenagers to help their parents grow.

I suspect, as God started to work with Jonah, the prophet was under the impression he already was a loving person: Look at how I've helped the Israelites. Look at what I've done to serve King Jeroboam. Look at all my accomplishments!

But as soon as God asked Jonah to love in a risky or dangerous way, his love evaporated, and he ran away. Jonah could no longer pretend to be a loving person. The truth was exposed.

The first step God takes to cultivate voluntary love in the heart of a rebel is to expose his or her lack of love for anyone but self. This is the step parents of teens must take in cultivating love in the hearts of their children. Ask their adolescents to love in ways that will expose their inability to love—their helplessness to be loving people apart from God's grace.

Why is it hard for teenagers to love?

Let's consider Jonah. Jonah is a symbol. He's an individual who's singled out by God as a representative of the whole nation of Israel.

God had grown frustrated with this generation of Israelites. He had set them apart to be a light to all the other nations. They were to love the rest of the world and show the world the way to God.

Instead Israel had become self-absorbed. Israelites cared only about themselves. In this book of Jonah, God takes one man—a spiritual leader, a prophet of God—and shows how hard it is even to get this great leader to love, let alone the whole nation.

Why was it so hard to get Jonah to love, and why is it so hard to get our kids to love voluntarily? Second Kings 14:23–27, tells what was going on with Israel at the time of Jonah's ministry. It's the same thing that goes on in each new generation.

> In the fifteenth year of Amaziah son of Joash king of Judah, Jeroboam son of Jehoash king of Israel became king in Samaria, and he reigned forty-one years. He did evil in the eyes of the LORD and did not turn away from any of the sins

of Jeroboam son of Nebat, which he had caused Israel to commit. He was the one who restored the boundaries of Israel from Lebo Hamath to the Sea of the Arabah, in accordance with the word of the LORD, the God of Israel, spoken through his servant Jonah son of Amittai, the prophet from Gath Hepher.

The LORD had seen how bitterly everyone in Israel, whether slave or free, was suffering; there was no one to help them. And since the LORD had not said he would blot out the name of Israel from under heaven, he saved them by the hand of Jeroboam son of Jehoash.

Notice that the word used to describe Ninevah is the same word that is used to describe this generation of Israelites. Ninevah was a "wicked" city, and Israel, during this period of time, was being ruled by a "wicked" king who was inciting the Israelites to live "wickedly." We're talking about two wicked nations that were in the same boat.

Despite the fact that this king was wicked, he was the one who restored the boundaries. Normally, Israel's wickedness led to lost territory. But in the grace of God, this time Israel expanded in spite of its wickedness. Jonah was working alongside this wicked king. The two of them were getting credit for the growth of Israel.

Why did God allow the nation of Israel to experience growth even though it was wicked? You've seen people who aren't living godly lives at all—in fact, maybe the exact opposite—but God seems to be blessing them. Their income, their fortune, their families seem to be prospering.

Why? Verse 26 gives us the answer. God chose, out of His grace and His compassion, to bless these people even though they weren't living for Him. He chose to do that because He loved them. But He went one step further and told Jonah that what He'd been doing for wicked Israel, He wanted to do also for wicked Ninevah.

Can we imagine how the conversation might have gone between God and Jonah?

"Jonah, will you go and help me love these people?"

"No way! I'm not going to go love our enemies. They deserve judgment"—as if his own people didn't. We see what makes it so hard for Jonah to love others. He lacked several qualities that are foundational to the ability to love others. It's as impossible for our kids to love as it was for Jonah until those qualities are developed.

What teens need to become loving

The first and foremost quality that love requires is **self-awareness**, awareness that in some fundamental way we are just like the people we've been asked to love. The more we perceive others to be different from us the more excuses and justification we find not to love them.

Recently, an adult encouraged a teenage girl to go up and welcome some visitors in her Sunday school class. Her response was, "Well, nobody did that for me when I was new in this class! If I didn't get it they shouldn't either. Besides, I don't know how to talk to those kinds of people."

We see the same kind of reasoning going on in Jonah's mind: Until the Ninevites start living like us, they deserve judgment. They certainly don't deserve your blessing, God.

Jonah showed no awareness that God viewed the Ninevites and the Israelites as equally wicked and as equally worthy of redemption. Jonah felt superior. People who feel superior to others have little self-awareness and make poor lovers.

They don't understand that we're all hurting in the same ways.

Jonah and his fellow citizens didn't realize that both the Israelites and the Ninevites were objects of God's love. Both peoples had the same need and desire to be loved. Neither of them deserved better treatment than the other.

To truly love requires a level of self-awareness that Jonah didn't have. It requires a level of self-awareness that most teenagers have not developed and may never develop without assistance from their parents.

Secondly, love always requires **self-exposure**. When we move out to love others, we may be doing something which no one else in the crowd is doing. We may be exposed as the only ones choosing to love. That's why it's often a lonely choice. It often produces criticism from someone.

Israelites were not good at loving their enemies. But God was asking Jonah to be different, to come out from the crowd, and be the one Israelite who would expose himself willing to love his enemies.

Jonah could imagine the consequences—social ostracism, the end of his career and ministry, possibly even imprisonment and death.

Crowds seldom encourage people to love. They mostly encourage people to hate. Whenever we make the choice to love we have to step out from the crowd and expose ourselves as different. We can't be conformists if we want to love. Conformists give in to pressure. Any love they show is forced.

Kathryn and Dirty Dawn

Kathryn went on a week-long missionary trip to an inner city mission with her church youth group. She really didn't want to but her parents made her go.

All week the kids got involved in a lot of "loving" activities. The leaders kept them busy. If someone was sitting around, a leader would say, get up there and hammer that board, or, sweep that floor. Do that, or, do this.

Sure, it was forced love. But these trips have some value because even forced love gives the kids a taste of the rewards of self-sacrifice. Hopefully, that will get them to the point where they will voluntarily want to love.

That's what happened with Kathryn. This girl had practically been dragged on the trip. The youth leaders had to nearly lasso her to get her into the activities at first. But things so changed that by the end of the trip she was at an all-time high.

The experience of loving people was the most rewarding and exciting thing that had ever happened to her. Only a few days after returning home she went to the youth pastor with a request.

"I've decided because of the trip that I want to be a missionary."

The youth pastor was floored. "You want to be a missionary?"

"Yes. I want to know what I need to do to prepare, because I would like to go to Europe this summer as a short-term missionary. What do I do to prepare for that?"

After absorbing the shock, the youth pastor replied, "OK, here's how you prepare. You know Dawn?"

"You mean Dirty Dawn?"

"Well, yes. It's your job to love her."

"Nobody likes Dawn. She smells. She's obnoxious. Do you know that three years ago she earned a trophy at school and she still carries it to church every Sunday in a paper sack? All you have to do is look at her and she wants to show you her trophy. Do you know how she dresses? She probably only washes her hair once a year!"

"Then why don't you teach Dawn how to take care of herself? Why don't you teach her how to wear makeup, how to dress? If the kids got together and voted on who was the sharpest looking girl in the youth group, it would be you. It only makes sense that you should be the one."

Kathryn was stumped. She didn't want to expose herself this way. When she was on the trip to the inner city everybody was loving; self-exposure wasn't required of her. But in a situation like this, if she chose to love on her own she was going to have to stick her neck out.

When Kathryn left his office that day, the youth pastor thought that her interest in missions would be short-lived.

But she surprised him. She made the decision to love Dirty Dawn.

Without anyone telling her to do so, she invited Dawn over to spend the night. She started teaching Dawn how to keep herself well-groomed, how to make and treat friends, how to be socially acceptable. Within a month there was such an incredible change in Dawn that the other kids began to want to hang around with this girl who used to be the group joke—all because Kathryn took the time to love her. And it was a voluntary love on Kathryn's part, a love that required self-exposure at first. Voluntary love always requires that—something Jonah wasn't willing to do, but something teenagers can learn when challenged to do so.

Another quality love requires is **self-denial**.

Let's use two circles to illustrate this quality. The inner circle represents our comfort, or safety, zone. The outer circle represents our danger, or discomfort, zone.

A decision to love is a decision to deny ourselves the privilege, the luxury, and the right to stay in the comfort zone. It is a conscious decision to move into the danger zone. The decision to love means a decision to face some kind of danger, or discomfort, for the sake of another person.

We can be forced to move out of our safety zones temporarily. But that's not denying ourselves comfort. It's self-protection. We're doing it because we don't want to be punished. (If you won't drive your brother to practice, I'll ground you for a week!)

Self-denial is when a person chooses voluntarily to deny himself comfort or safety and move into the danger zone in order to love somebody.

Jesus said, If you want to follow me, deny yourself, take up your cross and follow me (Matt. 16:24). We can't love without self-denial.

Jonah wasn't willing to do that. Think about how comfortable he was in the king's palace, a part of the royal court. He was a prophet who had a very popular message in his day. And here he was being commanded to move out of his comfort zone and go to Ninevah.

This is about as deep into the danger zone as he could go. Not only would it be dangerous because the Ninevites saw him as an enemy, but he would also be thought of as a traitor by his own people.

God was asking him to make a choice to deny himself, but he decided to run as far away as he could get in the opposite direction.

Patti's big finish

A lot of teens do the same thing. Patti was a girl riveted to the center of her safety zone. She was in the all-time Top Ten of kids who might be described as quiet, shy, and passive. When teens choose these qualities to stay safe, they show little willingness to move into the danger zone to love. As with most of these kinds of kids, there was a history behind Patti's decision to play it safe. As a little girl she was fearless—a very colorful personality in the neighborhood, a wonderful, outgoing child.

However, when she was eight she was molested by a baby-sitter. The incident was so traumatic, and Patti felt so ashamed about it, she became a different person. She became closed, guarded—afraid to trust anyone, afraid to let anyone get close to her.

In high school, Patti was befriended by some of the adult leaders in her church's youth program. Eventually they got past the walls she had erected and they learned the reason for her shyness.

Over several months, they helped her develop an awareness of how she had allowed the molestation to shape her personality. They helped her realize many children are victimized in some way, and all face the same challenge—finding their lives in God, even if the same kind of thing happens again.

They challenged her to open up to others and expose to them what God was doing in her heart. Little by little, she ventured out. Briefly she would extend herself to greet a new teen at the church—then she would withdraw. After years of keeping silent during discussions, she got so she would occasionally ask a question—then retreat. For awhile she ran out of her safety zone, only to run right back in after a few minutes. But to really become the loving person God wanted her to be, she needed to come out and live in the danger zone as a way of life.

The real breakthrough happened in an unexpected way. At Patti's school the seniors were going on a retreat at the end of the last week of classes. In response to a general appeal by her class adviser, Patti volunteered to give a talk at the retreat on How I've Grown During My Senior Year.

After she signed up, she couldn't believe what she had done. She was so nervous about it she could hardly sleep the entire week before the retreat. She thought about backing out, but chose not to because she believed there was something God wanted her to say.

At the retreat she was assigned to give her talk to her classmates one-third at a time—on three consecutive afternoons. This was incredible! Other seniors couldn't believe that the shyest kid in their class had volunteered to get up and speak to all of them.

For the first time she publicly told anybody that she had been molested as a little girl, how it affected her, and that she was hospitalized in junior high school when she had attempted suicide. And how she had found the love and strength in Jesus Christ to go on and find joy again by loving others.

Everybody sat in stunned silence as she talked. Although some of these kids had known Patti since elementary school, this was the first time any of them had heard her speak about herself, her struggles, and her relationship with Christ.

After she talked the first afternoon, nobody said a thing to her. She felt like a leper. She went out to a nearby woods and cried, thinking, This is the stupidest thing I have ever done. I've just made a complete fool of myself. How can I possibly do it again tomorrow?

After hardly sleeping, and not being able to eat, and feeling like a complete freak, somehow she got up and gave her talk the next day.

The reaction the second day was very similar to that of the first. Her classmates were very quiet again. The rest of that day, nobody said anything to her about what she had said.

Again, she felt incredible pain. But, unbelievably, she made herself get up and do it again the third day.

She told herself, At least I'm going to leave this afternoon on the bus. That will be it! I'll never have to see these people again. I'll just go home and crawl back into my shell and never come out again.

However, as she got up to speak that third day, she noticed that there were a lot more people there. Almost the whole senior class had shown up—most of the kids who were there the first two afternoons had come to hear her again. This time, while she was speaking, a number of the kids began to tear up. After her talk was over, nearly every person came up, threw their arms around her, and thanked her for telling her story. They told her of similar incidents in their lives. Several asked, "Do you think God could do for me what He's done for you?" It was the most incredible experience she'd ever had. It felt like winning the Olympics!

Now that's what we call self-exposure and self-denial! Patti chose to love voluntarily and go outside her comfort zone.

When teenagers start to make these kinds of choices spontaneously and regularly we know they're becoming the kind of people God wants them to be.

Why is it so hard to move kids to the point where they're loving voluntarily and spontaneously? Because it requires three things that most don't have: self-awareness, self-exposure, and self-denial.

When kids aren't growing in the development of these three qualities, they're going against God's design. They're operating as rebels—just as Jonah did. It's imperative that parents recognize this and know the forms this rebellion takes, because in their hearts all kids are rebels.

The four faces of adolescent rebellion

Rebellion is nothing more than the refusal to love the way God has asked us to love. What was Jonah rebelling against when God said, Go to Ninevah? He didn't want to love.

Anytime someone goes outside God's moral boundaries, on some level it's a refusal to love.

Some forms of adolescent rebellion are easy to recognize. Others are a little bit harder.

The most common face of adolescent rebellion is outright **defiance**. When we're asked to love we say no—just as Jonah did at first. Every parent frequently asks his or her kids to love: Would you love the rest of the family and vacuum the house? No—it's not fair that I should have to vacuum because

I was the last one to do it. It should be someone else's turn now.

That's defiance—an outright no. But this isn't always the first form that kids try.

The second face of rebellion is **compliance**. Jonah resorted to this as his second attempt at rebellion. After he was thrown off the ship in the middle of the storm, he was swallowed by a big fish. Then he said, I will comply now, God. Don't let me die. I'll do it.

Without further protest he went and preached to the Ninevites. But after he preached what did he do? He went up on a hillside and pouted. People who are forced to love pout afterwards.

The compliant kid says, "OK—if I have to I will." Underneath he's still a rebel.

Do you remember the elder brother of the prodigal son? He's the one who stayed home and cooperated while his brother was out being foolish. He's the one who said yes to all his father's requests. He was there all the time, complying, while his brother was away. But his true motives were exposed when his father threw a party for his prodigal brother, and he said, I've stayed here and I've complied all these years and you never threw a party for me.

Do you hear love under that statement? No; you hear somebody who loved because he believed that was the way to get the party.

OK, if that's the way I'm going to get my inheritance— by staying home—then I'll go ahead and do everything I'm supposed to do. That way, I'll get what I want.

That is forced love. A lot of times we mistakenly think that if we can get our kids just to comply, then we'll have great kids—just the kind that God wants.

But God isn't after compliance. He's not after forced

love. People who say, I'll do it if I have to, are still under-ground rebels. It's like the little boy who said, I'll sit down if you make me, but on the inside I'm still standing up.

A third face of rebellion is **impotence**. A kid who uses this says, I'm unable to do what you ask because I don't have the power to do what you ask. I'm not able.

Remember when God asked Moses to move outside his comfort zone in the wilderness and go back to Egypt? What did Moses say? I can't do it. I don't have the speaking voice, God. I can't, I can't, I can't. And God kept responding by offering what Moses lacked. But Moses continued to plead impotence. Finally, after God had offered him everything he conceivably needed to be successful, the true nature of Moses' heart came out. He resorted to defiance. That's when God became angry with him (see Exod. 3:1– 4:17).

Almost always, kids have one favorite face of rebellion they use as their primary strategy. When that doesn't work, they resort to a backup to avoid having to love.

Moses used impotence first, then resorted to defiance. Jonah used defiance, then resorted to compliance.

There's a fourth face of underground rebellion parents must be aware of: **negligence**. Negligence is usually pack-aged in one simple phrase: Oh, I forgot.

"Did you vacuum?"

"Where's my head—I forgot."

This may be the most effective strategy of all since it is the hardest one for parents to expose. Kids love it, because it gets them out of doing what they don't want to do—without having to face the serious consequence of outright defiance.

God says, I desire voluntary love. When He calls our kids to love, they may say, no, I shouldn't have to do that (defiance). They may say, if I have to (compliance). They may say, I can't (impotence). Or they might say, oh, I was going to, but I got busy and forgot (negligence).

These are the different strategies kids use, the different faces they put on to avoid the responsibility of loving. Each is worn over a rebellious heart.

The task we have in parenting teenage rebels is the same task God had in parenting Jonah—expose them as rebels and motivate them to change.

What won't work

When a parent undertakes the task of motivating a rebellious teen to love, he quickly finds out what won't work.

Commanding them

The first thing that won't work is merely commanding them to love: Now while I'm gone I want you to love your sisters; don't talk to your brother like that; be nice; share; be kind.

By commanding, we may be able to temporarily force our kid to love. From time to time, we might have to do just that to keep our kids from killing each other. However, we should never think we've accomplished our goal merely by forcing them to cooperate for a few hours. Commanding a person to love doesn't change his or her heart. Although God forced Jonah to go to Ninevah, it didn't change his heart. Afterwards he sat on the hill overlooking Ninevah and said, God, I don't know why you don't destroy those people. Jonah felt no love for anybody but himself. So, just commanding people to love doesn't change them.

Reasoning with them

The second thing that won't work with teenagers is reasoning with them, telling them why they ought to love. Sometimes we think the reason people don't love is they need to be educated. We say the reason why people treat each other in such dysfunctional ways is they just don't know better: If we could just put them in classes and teach them how to love; if we could just teach them how to relate; if we could just teach them communication exercises. Ignorance is the core problem!

According to the Bible, ignorance is not the core problem. The core problem is rebellion (see 2 Tim. 3:1–5). At the core we don't think we should have to love other people because we're too important for that. If I am at the center of the universe, why should I have to love anybody? They're supposed to love me. It only makes sense, if I'm the most important person in the world. A person can never be reasoned out of this kind of stubborn self-centeredness. The Apostle Paul warns not even to try (see 2 Tim. 2:23–26).

Threatening them

A third method of getting teens to love that doesn't work is threatening them. We can threaten them within an inch of their lives, but that won't be enough to get them to change. That may be enough to get them to comply temporarily but as soon as the person with the threatening words goes to the shopping center and leaves the kids alone, the love will evaporate.

Jonah complied after he was swallowed alive by a big fish, and sat in its gastric juices for three days. The threat of that happening again is enough to force anyone to love. But it is not enough to generate voluntary love. Jonah went and dutifully preached to the Ninevites. Afterwards it was still obvious he didn't love them in his heart.

When we set out to work with our kids we're not going to accomplish the work that God wants us to by ordering them to love, by giving them reasons to love, by threatening them with painful consequences if they don't love.

Please don't hear me saying that we shouldn't command them to love. Or that we shouldn't give them reasons to love. Or that we shouldn't enforce consequences if they don't love. But do hear me say that none of these steps in and of themselves, are enough to turn a self-centered rebel into a voluntary lover.

Six

Motivating a Teenage Rebel to Change

A man wanted to sell his car, and took it to a used-car salesman.

"Can you help me sell my car?"

"I don't know. What kind of mileage does it have on it?"

"Two hundred thirty thousand."

"There's no way we're going to sell a used car with two hundred thirty thousand miles. Roll the odometer back, then come and see me. Maybe we'll be able to sell it." The salesman expected his friend to return in a couple of days. However, weeks went by; his friend still hadn't returned. The salesman phoned him.

"Did you turn the odometer back?"

"Yes."

"Well then, when are you going to bring the car in?"

"I don't need to sell it now. It only has a hundred thousand miles on it."

That's what we call superficial change—changing the outer appearance of something without touching the inside. Most of what people do in the name of self-improvement is nothing more than this.

Easy to solve Sharon's problems

Sharon, a junior in high school, was bulimic and so depressed about her appearance she decided never to go to school again. Her parents were so concerned they sent her to a counselor at church. "Until I become a completely different person," she said, "I'm never going to set foot outside my door again." She told the counselor she was sick and tired of binge- ing and purging. She felt her life was one big game of pretend. She no longer wanted to be whoever others wanted her to be.

"I'm ready to change. I'm tired of being this fake per- son." Sharon and the counselor went to work. For three weeks they worked hard at uncovering the roots of her insecurities. However, the fourth week she didn't show for her appointment.

The counselor called her. "What happened, Sharon, where are you?"

"Well, I meant to call you with the good news. I don't need counseling any more."

"You don't?"

"No. All the problems we were working on have been solved. I'm back at school, I'm enjoying life—thanks a lot for the counseling."

The counselor was puzzled; What did we cover in those three weeks that revolutionized this girl's life? "Since your whole life is different, what do you think caused the change?"

"Well, I lost five pounds. That changed everything. A boy started liking me and gave me a phone call. Now we're going together and things are great!"

That's like turning the odometer back. She still had the same engine underneath the hood but made a superficial change to make it seem better.

When we talk about motivating rebellious teens to change, superficial change isn't what we want. We're talking about helping kids change on the inside. How do we do this?

Jonah's still mad

Once again, let's use the way God parented Jonah as our model. In Jonah, chapter 4, the prophet was used by God to lead the whole city of Ninevah into a change of heart, turning them from their wicked ways to embrace the one true God. When God saw this, He mercifully withheld the judgment He had threatened. This upset Jonah, however, revealing that he still had a rebellious heart that refused to love.

> "O LORD, is this not what I said when I was still at home? That is why I was so quick to flee to Tarshish. I knew that you are a gracious and compassionate God, slow to anger and abounding in love, a God who relents from sending calamity. Now, O LORD, take away my life, for it is better for me to die than to live."
>
> But the LORD replied, "Have you any right to be angry?" (Jonah 4:2–4).

In the first three chapters of the book of Jonah, we've seen God working with the prophet, but by the last chapter he's still not at the point where he displays voluntary love. He went to Ninevah and preached, but his heart wasn't in it. He wasn't loving the Ninevites like God wanted him to.

If God has a difficult time motivating a rebel to change, what kind of difficulty are we going to have motivating our rebellious adolescent children? This kind of change can only be accomplished by God when a person turns to Him and asks that his heart be changed.

King David expressed this in Psalm 51:10–13.

> Create in me a pure heart, O God,
>> and renew a steadfast spirit within me.
> Do not cast me from your presence
>> or take your Holy Spirit from me.
> Restore to me the joy of your salvation
>> and grant me a willing spirit, to sustain me.
> Then I will teach transgressors your ways,
>> and sinners will turn back to you.

David recognized that he would never be able to love

others—teach transgressors and turn them back to God—until he first had a pure heart. But he knew it was something he couldn't create on his own. God had to do it. That's why he was bringing his heart to God and asking Him for a new one. How can we motivate our children to do the same thing, to go to God and cry out, Create in me a pure heart?

Principles of helping teens change

The question we are asking is how on earth do we get someone who starts out like Jonah to end up like David? There are three principles to remember when attempting to do this.

Principle #1: No kid will ever ask God for a new heart until he first becomes aware that there's something desperately wrong with his old one.

Does that make sense? When do we go looking for a new car? Usually when we become aware there is something desperately wrong with our old car.

When does a person go shopping for a new heart? When he becomes aware that there is something desperately wrong with his old one.

Let's face facts. A kid has no conscious awareness of how bad his heart really is. Most kids operate under the assumption that they're pretty good.

For a fact, most parents attempt to operate under this assumption, too, until their kids do something really ugly that disproves it once and for all: How can it be possible that my kid could do something that ugly?

The hearts that our kids start out with contain some pretty bad and ugly things. And when bad and ugly things flow out of their hearts it shouldn't amaze us. What should amaze us is that it doesn't happen more.

Why didn't this ugly stuff come out before adolescence? Adolescence is when what's inside our kids spills out while parents are still around to deal with it.

> *Principle #2:* The most effective way to create an awareness in an adolescent that there is something desperately wrong with his heart is to catch him in the act of being a moral failure.

Another way of saying it: catch him in the act of failing to love. C. S. Lewis wrote in *Mere Christianity:* "No one knows how bad he is until he has tried very hard to be good and fails."

Moral failure in a teen often is the first step God uses to motivate him to change. Seeming tragedies like teenage pregnancies, school expulsion, and drug arrests, are very often the soil from which true spiritual life blossoms.

Many of the great men and women of God in the Bible blossomed spiritually in the wake of moral failure. Their failure helped them see how much they needed God.

Mission trip to Alaska

A few years ago our church took a group of high school seniors to work with the Native Americans in Alaska. When the plane set down in Anchorage, the kids were so excited! They were ready to really love the Native Americans.

Two-by-two the kids were sent into Native American neighborhoods to make contacts for a new church. This was during the season in Alaska known as "breakup time." That's when the snow pack is thawing, producing rivers of slush, mud, and dirty water. We sank into the snow as we went door-to-door. Cars splashed mud on us as they drove past. The students quickly grew cold, wet, and messy. And on top of it all, they weren't getting many warm receptions at the homes they were visiting.

It was getting harder and harder to love as the days went on. The kids' commitment to love was being severely tested.

About this time, we took the entire team away for a few days to the campus of a Bible college. The officials at the college agreed to host our kids while we were visiting some mission sites, if we agreed to honor their curfews. About 2:00 a.m., long after the adult leaders were fast asleep, a snowball fight erupted in the dorm hallways between our kids and some of the college students. The whole student body was awakened—just what the administration had asked us not to do.

The next morning those of us leading the team knew our kids' disregard for the school's rules had to be addressed. At a team meeting we brought up their actions of the night before for discussion. I'll never forget their reaction.

"What's the big deal? It was just a snowball fight! So what if we disrupted things a little? It was harmless fun."

What sounded like harmless fun to the kids smelled like defiance to the leaders. We brought them on the trip to teach them about loving others. Now the whole mission of the trip seemed threatened.

We forgot that often the first step in teaching people to love is catching them in the act of not loving. How else will they discover that something is wrong with their hearts?

Here it was—a great opportunity, but we didn't recognize it at first. Initially, all we wanted to do was strangle those kids for making us look bad!

However, as we sat and talked for several hours with them, the most valuable episode of the whole trip occurred. As we realized how hardhearted these kids were we began to weep.

That's when their attitudes began to soften and they began to do some soul searching, seeing first-hand the pain their defiance had caused. It changed their entire outlook. Their defiance no longer seemed like harmless fun. It seemed ugly. They became brokenhearted over their own disrespect and rudeness—a necessary step toward being motivated to change. Many of these kids later commented that this was one of the most significant events in their spiritual development during their high school days. It was the first time anyone had made them take a long, hard look at themselves—the ugly part!

Certainly the most effective way to create awareness in an adolescent of what's wrong with his heart is to catch him in the act of failing to love and to discuss it with him.

The most important decision?

> Principle #3: When a teen becomes aware that he's not very good at loving (There's something wrong with my heart!), he faces a critical choice: Do I stay this kind of person, or do I change?

This will be perhaps the most important decision of his entire life.

It's a choice that every parent has to make, as well, when his lovable child is transformed—almost overnight—into a rebellious adolescent.

I rather think that adolescence is a time bomb God plants in each of our homes. In our middle years, just when we think we have life all figured out—and perhaps have grown complacent about our own spiritual growth—the bomb goes off. Our children are transformed into teenagers. Nothing that worked when we parented them as children works anymore. Our resources to love them become exhausted.

We become aware that we don't have the ability within ourselves to love a disrespectful and defiant teenager. It's our opportunity to turn to God, as David did, and ask Him to create pure hearts in us—the kind that can even love an obnoxious teenager.

At one time in my youth ministry I was challenged for not having a heart of love when handling teenagers.

Mechanic—or friend?

"I've watched you work with kids," said this friend.

"You're very careful around the kids. You say all the right things, but something is missing. It's as if you are working on an assembly line. The kids are the pieces that are coming along on a conveyor belt. You pick them up, do an operation, put them back on the belt, and they go by. The work you do with them is precise, but I don't see you becoming personally involved with them.

"You're more like their mechanic than their friend."

That feedback hit me like a ton of bricks. There was a ring of truth to it. I'd learned early in my life there were some real advantages to not getting personally involved with people. It avoids a lot of conflict. But it also severely limits the impact one can have on people's lives.

I didn't want to be a people-mechanic. I didn't want to be that kind of person any longer. I wanted to change. But how? I decided to work hard at being more personable.

After a little while I got some feedback from the kids. They thought I was going overboard, trying too hard to be friendly. I was coming across as a fake.

So I decided to concentrate on being more sincere. Next thing I knew the kids were telling me I was being syrupy.

After trying three or four different things—all with similar results—I went back to my friend.

"What am I going to do? You've pointed this out, that I operated like a mechanic. I've tried all these different things but they don't seem genuine. What can I do to change?"

I'll never forget his response.

"Well, if you could change this on your own, you wouldn't need God."

It had never occurred to me that this was something only God could change. Something was wrong with my heart. It was as if it were encased in plastic. I couldn't be warm to people without being fake. Turning to God was my only hope for change.

In time, as I asked Him to create a new heart in me, the Spirit of God began to melt the plastic and free me to genuinely love. Sure, there are parts of the plastic that are still there. But when I see them surface, I've learned to race to God because I know I can't change on my own.

Getting teens to run to God

We want to guide our teens to do the same thing. Once they become aware of how incapable their hearts are of truly loving we want them to run to God.

The Bible uses the word *broken* to describe a person who has seen his heart as it really is and doesn't want to go on like that.

The Bible describes it as being "brokenhearted." What is broken in this kind of person is the determination to go on being an unloving person. The opposite is a person like Jonah. As the book closes, Jonah is not yet a brokenhearted man. He still feels superior to the Ninevites. He feels justified in his refusal to love them. His determination to be a rebel has not been broken.

Sharon, the girl who had bulimia, felt very ashamed about her behavior. She went to great lengths to keep anyone from finding out about it. Despite the guilt, however, she had very little desire to change.

It's important not to confuse brokenness with just feeling guilty or ashamed about something. There's a big difference between wanting to hide something and wanting to change it.

After David committed adultery with Bathsheba and murdered Uriah, he felt guilt and shame. He covered it up. He hid it, but he didn't cry out to God to change his heart until later—when brokenness developed. When our teens become aware there is something desperately wrong with their hearts and want to change—like David did—then we can say they're brokenhearted.

Two motivational factors

There are two factors that must be cultivated before an adolescent will ever seek God for a new heart. Factor number one is awareness of his failure to love. And factor number two is brokenness over his failure to love.

These two factors form a helpful model in understanding the stages kids move through in their spiritual development. On the matrix below, the vertical scale represents how much awareness a kid has of his failure to love—how much awareness he has of his own self-centeredness. The horizontal scale represents brokenness—how much his determination to be a selfish person has been broken. The four quadrants of the matrix depict the four stages every kid must pass through to become the loving kind of person God wants him to be.

Stage one: ignorant rebel

In the first stage, found in the *upper left quadrant* of the matrix, he is an ignorant rebel. In this stage, the adolescent has no awareness that he's failing to love and, of course, no brokenness about it. How can you be broken about something that you're not even aware of?

This is where Jonah was in chapter 1 of the book of Jonah. He thought he was a committed, dedicated servant of God. He thought he was doing all these things for God. He had no idea how rebellious his heart really was—how committed it was to not go out of the safety zone. This is the stage in which all of our kids start out.

Take an eighteen-year-old boy named Bret. Bret was having trouble being respectful toward his parents. He lived

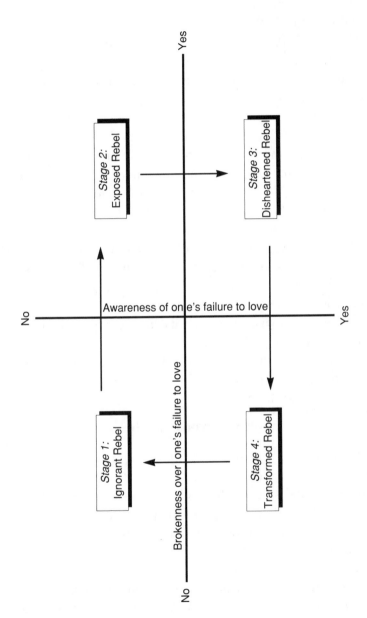

Stages of a Teenager's Spiritual Development

with his mother and a stepfather. And he spent every other weekend with his dad and stepmother.

Bret had a lot of anger toward his parents for several reasons. He was mad at them for the marriage breaking up and because they said a lot of negative things about each other in front of him.

He was also angry at them because he couldn't get the time or attention from them that he wanted. He felt jealous at home around his mom because she was giving most of her attention to his stepfather. And he felt ignored and neglected when he visited his dad on the weekends. He showed his anger through defiance and negligence. He wanted to hurt them as they had hurt him.

Yet he had very little awareness of how unloving and selfish his behavior was. It seemed reasonable and justifiable under the circumstances. If you asked him if he loved his parents, he would argue that he did.

Although we wish that kids like Bret could move from stage one right to stage four where they would be different, it doesn't happen like that. Just as Jonah or David or the prodigal son didn't, our kids won't, either, without going through some intermediate stages.

Stage two: exposed rebel

At stage two, depicted in the *upper right quadrant*, they become exposed rebels. They become aware that they are in opposition to God's design for their lives—but as yet feel no brokenness about it. The exposed rebel says, Yeah, I know I'm not doing what they want me to do. I know I'm being rotten in some ways, but I don't care. I'm justified in living the way I'm living.

Jonah moved to this stage when he fled God and sailed to Tarshish. This was a step of growth for Jonah, just as it can be for our kids.

Moving a rebel from a place in which he is ignorant of his condition to a point in which he's aware of his rebellion and knows it is a conscious choice, is always growth. Jesus said, "I know your deeds, that you are neither cold nor hot. I wish you were either one or the other! So, because you are lukewarm—neither hot nor cold—I am about to spit you out of my mouth" (Rev. 3:15–16).

When a teen is an ignorant rebel, he is lukewarm. When a teen moves away from lukewarmness, his first stopover is to become cold. This is stage two. It's much easier to deal with someone who's cold than with someone who's lukewarm. That's why Jesus said that He'd rather people were cold than lukewarm. When they're cold, they know their hearts aren't with God. They can't pretend, like lukewarm people do.

When our teens move to stage two, it scares us into thinking we must be doing something wrong. If this is the case then God must have done something wrong with Jonah. For Jonah turned cold.

He didn't seem so cold at the start of the book. He was serving Israel as a prophet. Although he only loved those who loved him, at least he thought he was serving God. By the end of the book, we find Jonah sitting up on a mountain, depressed and wanting to die. At least now he knew how far his heart was from God. That could be the first step toward transformation.

Although stage two is tough for parents to endure, it can be even tougher to explain to friends. Can you hear it at church?

The teacher asks, "Any prayer requests or praise today?"

And I stand up and say, "Yes! We'd like to praise the Lord! Our son got arrested this week.

"You know, for the longest time he was just going through the motions, coming to church, kind of fitting into the crowd, looking like he was a pretty good Christian, but we knew there was something wrong underneath. And we praise the Lord it's now out in the open.

"We're glad now he has to face the fact that his heart is capable of actually stealing something. We see this as a step of growth for this boy."

How would the Sunday school class react? Would they see it as a step of growth?

Often when the Spirit of God is working in somebody's life, we mistake it as a step backward. Moving a kid from stage one to stage two is a prerequisite to maturity. However, God never intended for anyone to stay there.

Stage three: disheartened rebel

At stage three, shown in the *lower right quadrant*, he becomes a disheartened rebel. Stage three is the position in which a teen has both an awareness of what he is and a brokenness about it: That's not the kind of person I want to be. I can't believe I've hurt people the way I have. I can't believe I've been so selfish. I want to change.

At this point, he hasn't changed yet. He may still be behaving in some ways as a rebel. But he's unhappy about it when he does. He has lost hope that being a rebel will ever work—will ever really get him what he wants in life.

Whether he ever moves to stage four or not depends on what he does to change. If he attempts to rehabilitate himself, he'll remain stuck at stage three—or drift back to an earlier stage.

However, if he approaches God with his broken heart and asks for help, he will progress to stage four.

Stage four: transformed rebel

At stage four, in the *lower left quadrant*, he will become a transformed rebel. This is where every Christian parent should desire his or her teen to be. It's the stage at which transformation of the heart occurs. In response to a broken-hearted rebel's prayers, God creates in him a heart that is equipped to genuinely love.

However, no one stays here very long, either. It's questionable how long anyone can stay at this stage. A person at stage four tends to drift to stage one.

Maybe Jonah was at stage four before the book opens, but stopped looking at his own heart and slowly drifted to becoming an ignorant rebel again. Spiritual growth is cyclical. People start at stage one, move to stage two, three, and sometimes four. But they drift back into earlier stages and must begin the growth process over again.

Our job is to help our kids go through the cycle at least once by the time they are out of high school. This will equip them to go through the stages on their own as they get to be independent adults.

Three motivational blocks

At each of these stages there are blocks that prevent a rebel from growing and moving on to the next stage. We might call them motivational blocks.

Avoiding responsibility for loving other people
For example, avoiding responsibility for loving other people is the block that keeps a person from moving from stage one to stage two. Kids allowed to avoid responsibility for loving others stay stuck at stage one. We never find out how bad we are at loving until we have the responsibility of loving someone. Unfortunately, the first time people find out they're not very good at loving is when they get married. It is sad that people can get this far without having had to wrestle with the selfish condition of their own

hearts. This, of course, leaves them ill-equipped to genuinely love.

Inability to feel anybody else's pain

The inability to feel anybody else's pain but his own
keeps a kid from moving from stage two to stage three. When
Jonah sat up on the mountain and looked over Ninevah, he
was probably thinking, I have a right to be ticked off and mad
that You saved these people!

But God could have wondered, What am I going to do to
get Jonah to feel the pain of others?

Jonah was not feeling the pain of the Ninevites at all. He
was feeling no pain but his own. That's when God decided to
grow a tree over Jonah to give him some shade from the hot
sun. That comforted Jonah and made him feel better.

When God caused the plant to die, Jonah grew upset
again. God wanted Jonah to feel the same pain He was feeling. Jonah treasured the tree; in letting it die God was saying,
Can you feel My pain a little bit now Jonah? Can you feel the
pain I feel when something I treasure is lost? That's what
brings people to the point of brokenness—getting them to feel
someone else's pain, especially pain they caused.

Researchers have studied kids who murder, rape, and
commit other violent crimes. They've found the most effective
way to help these kids is to get them to feel someone else's pain.

Otherwise, the victim is like a thing to them, a piece of
furniture. If they want to use a piece of furniture or burn it up
they can because it doesn't have feelings.

In working with these kids, therapists require them to sit
and listen for hours to the pain of victims of crimes similar to
the ones they've committed.

The whole process might take twenty, fifty, or a hundred
hours. Sooner or later, these hard kids, exposed to the pain of
the victims of their own crimes, begin to break. Only after the

pain gets through do they finally begin to cry and to experience brokenness. They finally feel, I don't want to be this way, I don't want to hurt anybody like this again.

This is something every teen needs to experience to some degree before he can move from stage two to stage three. In Alaska, our teens moved from being ignorant rebels to being disheartened rebels only after they had to sit and listen for several hours to the injury they caused. As they saw our tears and heard our pain, there began to be some brokenness. Most of the time people don't have to face the consequences of their selfishness. They don't have to watch, or observe, or feel the pain that they cause by being unloving.

Bret—cold-blooded kid

Earlier in this chapter, we met Bret, the eighteen-year-old who was angry with his parents. He was as cold as they come. He felt no one's pain because he had shut himself off from his own pain. The fingers we use to touch our pain are the same ones we use to touch other people's pain. If I make my hand go numb so that I don't have to feel my pain, I won't be able to feel anybody else's pain, either. That's what Bret had done. No one thought he was reachable.

Then one day it happened. Bret was driving his motorcycle down the street. He was in a hurry, full of anger, when he came up behind a little eight-year-old girl on a bicycle.

Despite Bret honking his horn and yelling at the girl, she wouldn't move out of the way. She kept weaving back and forth across the street—always staying in front of him. Finally, he slammed the accelerator down and crashed into her.

She flew through the air and landed in a ditch.

Bret never stopped his motorcycle, or looked back. It took the police three hours to find him. They had to wrestle him down before arresting him for hit-and-run.

This was the event that made Bret finally admit that there was something wrong with his heart.

It turned out to be the opening everyone had been praying for.

He'd been a monster all along, but hadn't seen it. What changed? Something broke through and made him feel the pain of that child and her family as she lay bruised and broken in the hospital, facing an extended period of recovery.

Believing God doesn't want to be involved with his problems

The belief God doesn't want to be involved with them in the midst of their problems is the block that keeps our kids from moving from stage three to four, and is perhaps the hardest block to overcome.

When people become disheartened rebels they want to change the kind of people they are. They mistakenly think they have to do this themselves through self-discipline and self-improvement. They can't believe that God will do a work in their lives. They believe they have to clean themselves up before God will have anything to do with them.

Unbelief in God's grace keeps us from going to God, as David did in Psalm 51, and saying, God, will you create in me a clean heart?

How can we help our kids overcome this block? When Bret ran over this little girl he thought no one would want anything to do with him again. He figured his parents would give up on him, that he would never be welcomed at church again. He assumed that if he had been exposed as that ugly no one would ever want to have anything to do with him.

But Bret found out that wasn't true. There were many people who wanted to be involved with him—even though his ugliest parts had been exposed.

Giving kids a taste of God's grace, God's acceptance of them when their ugliest parts are exposed, helps clear away the last block that prevents them from becoming transformed rebels—unbelief in God's grace.

Seven

God's Example for Parenting Rebels

Parenting teens is a bad news/good news story.

The bad news is that every teenager is a rebel at heart. That's probably not too much of a surprise. Deep down, we know our teen isn't perfect. We know she's the same as every other person who walks this earth—morally flawed.

However, the good news is that direction for handling teenage rebellion is only seconds away. Seconds? Yes, seconds. Like, how long does it take to go find your Bible?

Are you surprised that the solution is so close at hand? Even those who read the Bible a lot are surprised that it has so much to say about teen rebellion.

Actually the Old Testament is a dramatic story of how God parented rebels and tried to guide them to the point where they would become transformed rebels. Look at Hosea, where the message of the Old Testament is summarized, in chapter 11. In verses 1–10, the Lord says,

When Israel was a child, I loved him,
>and out of Egypt I called my son.
But the more I called Israel,
>the further they went from me. . . .
It was I who taught Ephraim to walk,
>taking them by the arms;
but they did not realize
>it was I who healed them.

I led them with cords of human kindness,
>with ties of love;
I lifted the yoke from their neck
>and bent down to feed them.

Will they not return to Egypt
>and will not Assyria rule over them
>because they refuse to repent?. . .
My people are determined to turn from me. . . .

How can I give you up, Ephraim?
>How can I hand you over, Israel?
How can I treat you like Admah?
>How can I make you like Zeboiim?
My heart is changed within me;
>all my compassion is aroused.
I will not carry out my fierce anger,
>nor again devastate Ephraim.
For I am God, and not man—
>the Holy One among you.
>I will not come in wrath.
They will follow the LORD;
>he will roar like a lion.
When he roars,
>his children will come trembling from
the west

As a parent of a rebellious teen do you ever feel like God felt? When Israel was a child God loved him. God spared nothing in nurturing and guiding this kid. Yet, Israel was a stubborn rebel, determined to turn from God. But God didn't give up on Israel. He wasn't going to send him off to military school or put him up for adoption. Although His anger was aroused by His son's actions, He wasn't going to carry it out against him.

Reacting to rebellion

We nurture our children from infancy, diaper them, teach them how to walk, pick them up when they fall. We take them to the first day of school and meet them every day when they come home. We clothe them, feed them, wipe their tears away, rock them to sleep. We're there to kiss them as they wake up in the morning. We wash their clothes, even their bodies. After meeting all these needs, we're disappointed when, as they hit adolescence, they begin to rebel and to pull away from us. They become disrespectful. They defy us. Our disappointment turns to shock and our shock to outrage. Both compassion and anger fill our hearts at the same time.

That's what God felt toward Israel, both anger and compassion. But according to Hosea, God did not let His anger toward His "teen" control Him, as a human father would.

Like Him, we must be careful during our children's adolescence not to come to them in wrath instead of compassion. Even though we feel hurt, disappointment, and anger, we must not allow these feelings to cloud our judgment and dictate our actions. God's relationship with Israel is our model for how to love a kid who angers us. Following it will enable us to parent from love instead of anger.

In the previous chapter, we observed this model in God's dealings with Jonah. We observed the stages God tried to guide him through which were also the stages God guided Israel through. At each stage, God models what a parent needs to do to guide a rebel to the next stage. What a kid needs when he's an ignorant rebel is different than what he needs when he is an exposed rebel. What he needs when he is brokenhearted rebel is far different than what he needs when he is a transformed rebel. God shows how to parent rebels at each stage.

Parenting an ignorant rebel

In Malachi 3:6–13, we get insight into ignorant rebels and what they need:

I the LORD do not change. So you, O descendants of Jacob, are not destroyed. Ever since the time of your forefathers you have turned away from my decrees and have not kept them. Return to me, and I will return to you. . . .

But you ask, "How are we to return?"

Will a man rob God? Yet you rob me.

But you ask, "How do we rob you?"

In tithes and offerings. You are under a curse—the whole nation of you—because you are robbing me. Bring the whole tithe into the storehouse, that there may be food in my house. Test me in this . . . and see if I will not throw open the floodgates of heaven and pour out so much blessing that you will not have room enough for it. I will prevent pests from devouring your crops, and the vines in your fields will not cast their fruit. . . . Then all the nations will call you blessed, for yours will be a delightful land. . . .

You have said harsh things against me. . . .

Yet you ask, "What have we said against you?"

Israel is living in rebellion, but when God asks them to return to Him, the people play dumb. They say, "How are we to return?" It's as if they weren't aware at all of their spiritual condition. We're talking about rebels who were ignorant of the significance of their actions. They had no idea that withholding their offerings and tithes was a problem.

When God accused Israel of saying harsh things against Him, their answer is predictable.

"What have we said against you?"

Perhaps they're aware of the words they said but not aware of the significance of them.

Israel is an ignorant rebel at this point. He is unaware of the true nature and significance of his actions. He is treating high treason against the Lord of the universe as if it were a misdemeanor. He had no idea of the impact and consequences of his actions.

An ignorant rebel is one who is unaware of the significance of the choice to get off God's track of truth. He may or may not be aware that he's choosing to leave the path, but he's certainly not aware of the significance of it. Each of the four faces of rebellion that we studied in chapter five help a rebel stay ignorant of the true nature of what he is doing.

The exposed rebel says, I'm not going to do what's expected without a fight. This can wear parents down. Finally, they throw their hands up and say, I'm done fighting. The kid's rebellion is never subdued. He remains a rebel because the parent has failed to teach him that the penalty for rebellion against God's moral order cannot ultimately be dodged.

The compliant rebel stays ignorant because he never does anything wrong in front of his parents. It's like prison. As long as the guards are there the inmate obeys and looks like a law-abiding citizen. One wonders why he needs to be in prison at all. The rebellion that is still in his heart often remains hidden until the guards are out of sight.

Impotence also helps kids stay ignorant of their rebellion. Kids can be masters at convincing their parents, and even themselves, that they shouldn't be expected to get their homework done.

"But Mom, can't I . . . ?"

Betty was like this. As soon as she came home from school each day, her mom told her, "Before you do anything else, do your homework."

"But, Mom can't I at least get a snack first? I've been in school all day."

"OK, but as soon as your snack is done, get right to work." So Betty got something out of the refrigerator, went in, and watched TV. Long after the snack was consumed, her mom came into the family room.

"Betty, get in there right now and do your homework."

"But, Mom, I'm in the middle of a show. Can't I at least finish it?"

"OK, but as soon as you finish that show, get your homework done." Just as the show ended, Betty got a phone call. Several minutes later Mom started pacing up and down, making hand signals to her daughter. Betty put her hand over the phone and whispered, "Mom, I can't be rude and hang up."

Mom again gave up and went in to fix supper. When Betty finally hung up and went out to the kitchen, her mother asked, "You haven't done your homework yet, have you?"

"You know I've been busy ever since I got home."

"Well, right after supper, do your homework."

"But, Mom, it's my turn to do the dishes tonight."

"I'll do the dishes for you. You go right to your room and do your homework." After supper Betty disappeared. Mom did the dishes, then went to check up on Betty. She found her in the shower.

"What are you doing in there? You're supposed to be doing your homework!"

"But Mom, you know I wash my hair on Thursday nights. I couldn't go to school with my hair the way it was."

Underneath all her actions what is Betty saying? She's saying, Mom, I can't handle all these responsibilities, all this stuff that's expected of me. You've got to keep making allowances for me.

So her mom kept making allowances, convinced that her daughter shouldn't be expected to obey. Betty's disobedience went unexposed for what it was—rebellion.

Betty had no idea of the significance of her actions. She had no idea she was a rebel and what the price of her rebellion eventually would be.

Negligence works very similarly to hide the true nature of a teen's rebellion. It hides rebellion behind the simple phrase, I forgot. Forgetfulness sounds so benign, hardly the kind of thing that gets dealt with severely. Although it may concern parents, it is often dismissed by them as a minor thing that carries little consequence.

How to parent the ignorant rebel

What does an ignorant rebel need the most? Although he wears many different faces—defiance, compliance, impotence, or negligence—what every ignorant rebel needs is to be made aware of the significance of his choices.

Most kids have no idea of the significance of their rebellion. Sure, they may know they're rebelling, but they think it's expected of them because they're teenagers. Sitcoms and movies portray outwitting your parents as a harmless game.

Eternal consequences are at stake
Kids have no idea that every choice they make as human beings has spiritual consequences. This is true because human beings are made in the image of God and are spiritual agents. Every time we decide to go outside the boundaries God has established it goes against our very design and robs us of our sense of liveliness and joy.

Any time we make a choice to promote the work of God we spread life. Anytime we make a choice to hurt the work of God we spread death. In both cases, we will reap what we sow.

Ever since Adam and Eve sinned in the Garden and death entered the world, there's been a war going on between the forces of spiritual life and the forces of spiritual death.

Kids have no idea, unless someone teaches them, that they are participants in this battle. Every time they make a choice to move off the pathway of truth they're making a choice to aid the forces of spiritual death.

Satan deceives adolescents into believing there is no price tag on rebellion. He wants them to think rebellion is something that can be done harmlessly, inexpensively, and without consequence.

That's not true. Everything people do has great significance—eternal significance. Rebellion should never be overlooked by parents. Teenagers only stay ignorant rebels when the adults in their world ignore their rebellion.

If what's most needed is to make our kids aware of the significance of their rebellion, how does a parent do it?

Learning to roar!

By roaring! That's right, we as parents must roar as God did in Hosea 11:10, "They will follow the LORD; he will roar like a lion. When he roars, his children will come trembling from the west."

What makes a rebel tremble? What makes him stop in his tracks and count the cost of what he's doing? It's going to be a roar.

In 1 Peter 5:8, we are warned that Satan is a roaring lion, prowling around—just off the path of truth.

In order to protect us, God roars, too. It's a roar of warning, however, not a roar of attack.

We must learn how to give warning roars to our kids. Whenever they begin to venture off the path God has laid out for them, we must warn them of the consequences. Regardless of how subtle the rebellion is or what face it wears, they must be warned of its spiritual significance.

How do we give this roar of warning to our rebellious teens? It begins with calling their rebellion to their attention.

In the verses quoted from Malachi, when Israel rebelled God plainly called it to their attention.

Similarly, the words we use to call problem behavior to our kids' attention must be clear and direct.

> When you say "I can't," it sounds like you are saying "I won't."
>
> When you say "I forgot," I wonder if what you really mean is that you don't think our requests are very important.
>
> When you say "no," it's a deliberate choice to go against our authority. Do you have any idea what consequences that will have?

Make no mistake, roaring requires strong words, because we are warning kids of strong danger. But it does not call for loud or violent words, because that constitutes an attack, the very thing we're trying to protect our kids from. A roar should warn kids of the significance and consequences of their choices should they continue their rebellion. It is designed to keep kids from getting off the path of truth and being attacked by Satan. It is not to be used by parents to attack their kids. This could do more damage than Satan could ever do.

Over and over again in the Old Testament we see God roaring at His rebellious children, Don't you understand the significance of what you are doing? The suffering you are causing to yourselves, your families, your children, and to your neighbors? Turn back before the consequences become even greater.

After giving a warning roar, parents should wait—stand guard, in a sense, on the shoulders of the path and wait until their teen again decides to get off the pathway of truth. When he does, he's no longer an ignorant rebel. Because of our roars, he's been made aware of the dangers. When he proceeds with his rebellion, he is an exposed rebel.

Parenting an exposed rebel

Parenting an exposed rebel is a different ball game than parenting an ignorant rebel.

An exposed rebel is someone who, despite the warning "roar" of his parent, is still determined to live off the track of God's truth. Although he's been made aware that rebellion has a price, he's thinking, I can find a way around this. I can figure out a way to avoid the consequences, a way to beat authority. There is a way I can get what I want without my parents getting in the way!

The exposed rebel usually can find a way to do this—at least temporarily. He doesn't believe the warning of his parents. He thinks, Violating God's moral order really isn't that big a deal. My parents don't know what they're talking about.

What does an exposed rebel need the most, then?

The exposed rebel needs to experience firsthand the natural consequences of his rebellion.

He needs to experience death, little deaths at first; then, as the rebellion continues, progressively larger and larger ones. This is the only way to turn a rebel into a believer.

In God's physical order, one becomes a believer in the law of gravity the first or second time he tries to defy it, because of the painful consequences. In God's moral order, the consequences of violating His law may not be as immediate. But they are just as inevitable.

Wise parents help their kids learn this by letting them experience "little deaths" as a consequence of their defiance. God did this with Jonah by depositing him in the stomach of a fish for three days.

A little death involves some type of loss for the rebel— usually the loss of freedom. It could mean losing the opportunity to go somewhere for the weekend: his rebellion led to the "death" of his plans for the weekend. Designing a little death takes some imaginative judgment on the part of the parents. Its severity should reflect the severity of the rebellious act. Its purpose is to persuade our kids that rebellion is expensive and ultimately results in the death of something they value.

Learning to wound

If the word we use to describe the way we parent an ignorant rebel is *roar*, then the word we use for parenting an exposed rebel is *wound*. When we deal with the exposed rebel, we are required out of love to wound him.

"Wounding" is arranging for the adolescent to experience first-hand the pain of a little death. It is clear that when rebellious Israel failed to listen to God's roar, His next step was to wound.

For I will be like a lion to Ephraim,
> like a great lion to Judah.
I will tear them to pieces and go away;
> I will carry them off, with no one to rescue
them.
Then I will go back to my place
> until they admit their guilt.
And they will seek my face. (Hos. 5:14–15)

Notice the purpose of the wounds God inflicts is to get the rebel to seek Him. Or, as Solomon put it in Proverbs 20:30, "Blows and wounds cleanse away evil."

Likewise, the wounds or little deaths a parent inflicts must have this same intent. That's why Solomon also said, "Wounds from a friend can be trusted" (Prov. 27:6).

Parenting the brokenhearted rebel

At stage three, the brokenhearted rebel needs something still different than what an ignorant or an exposed rebel needs.

Psalm 32:1–9 gives us a picture of David at this stage:

> Blessed is he
>> whose transgressions are forgiven,
>> whose sins are covered.
> Blessed is the man
>> whose sin the LORD does not count against
> him
>> and in whose spirit is no deceit.
>
> When I kept silent,
>> my bones wasted away
>> through my groaning all day long.
> For day and night
>> your hand was heavy upon me;
> my strength was sapped
>> as in the heat of summer.   *Selah*
> Then I acknowledged my sin to you
>> and did not cover up my iniquity.
> I said, "I will confess
>> my transgressions to the LORD"—
>> and you forgave
>>> the guilt of my sin.   *Selah*
>
> Therefore let everyone who is godly pray to you
>> while you may be found;
>> surely when the mighty waters rise,
>> they will not reach him.
> You are my hiding place;
>> you will protect me from trouble
>>> and surround me with songs of deliverance.
>>>> *Selah*
>
> I will instruct you and teach you in the way you
> should go;

I will counsel you and watch over you.
Do not be like the horse or mule,
which have no understanding
but must be controlled by bit and bridle
or they will not come to you.

Observe how God parents a brokenhearted David. It's important to remember that David got to this point because God wounded him first.

If parents aren't active in roaring or wounding, they may never get the opportunity to parent a brokenhearted teenager. Without help from parents, not many kids will reach this point.

In this passage, we can observe God offering David exactly what a brokenhearted rebel needs the most. A brokenhearted rebel needs to be brought near the One who can help him acquire a new heart.

This is tougher to do than one might think. A brokenhearted rebel can be like a horse that won't go to his master. Although he wants to change, he may mistakenly think he can make these changes himself. He may even think this is a prerequisite to being wanted by God or anybody else.

This is why brokenhearted rebels need help from their parents.

Learning to embrace

In the same way ignorant rebels need roars, and exposed rebels need wounds, brokenhearted rebels need to be embraced, as the father embraced the prodigal son when he returned home brokenhearted. This is what God offered David in Psalm 32.

When a teen is brokenhearted it is an ideal time to embrace him. Embraces are the most powerful in a kid's life at this stage. Embrace an exposed rebel and all it will do is reinforce his rebellious heart. But embrace a brokenhearted rebel and it teaches him something of God's grace.

What would have happened if the father of the prodigal son had gone after him when he was still living it up in the bars? The father would have been laughed at and mocked. His embrace would have been seen as weakness.

However, by waiting until the son reached stage three and then embracing him, his father was able to teach him a powerful lesson about grace. Embraces aren't very powerful when one's rebelliousness is intact. When his rebelliousness has been broken and his ugliness and self-centeredness have been exposed, an embrace can be very powerful.

Before we go on, it's important to clarify what we mean by "embrace." It's important to provide physical contact with our teens at all stages of rebellion. But an embrace is more than just a hug. It's more like a catch—catching them as they come running into our arms for help and mercy. This doesn't occur until stage three.

It is doubtful if a parent who has never been embraced will know how to embrace his or her kids.

Embracing, in the way we're using this word, is something that can only happen from one brokenhearted person to another. Arrogant people do not embrace. They give polite hugs. Only brokenhearted people know how to embrace. It's not one body hugging another body. Rather, it's one heart hugging another heart. And you know we can't hug a heart when it's an ice cube. Only when the ice has melted and the heart is warm, broken, and reaching out can it be embraced.

How can we know when it's time to embrace our rebellious son? We must wait until the adolescent expresses his brokenness in words. God tells His rebellious children to take words with them when they come to Him with a broken heart (Hos. 14:1–2).

Why is it important to wait for the rebel to express his

brokenheartedness in words? Until he says it, we don't know what is going on in his heart. We can observe outward behavior—depression, pouting, despair, and disillusionment—and mistake them for brokenness. We want to be sure it is brokenheartedness before we embrace him.

In another Old Testament book, Joseph's brothers came to him after their dad's death. They came looking sheepish, ashamed, and timid. Outwardly they appeared broken about selling Joseph into slavery when he was young, until they opened their mouths. They were only worried about protecting themselves from Joseph's anger. There was no brokenness, no expression of sorrow, no evidence of love for Joseph. That's why Joseph wept. They were still rebels. They weren't broken yet (see Gen. 50:15–21).

It's important to wait until our teens express their brokenness in words. Then we call them near us and embrace them.

We embrace them with our arms, our eyes, and our words. With all three, we tell them that they're valued and wanted by us. Even in their broken condition—even with their ugly parts exposed—we tell them we want to be near them.

Many parents might think at this point, This is it. Our kid is sorry for what he's done. He's come crying. We've hugged him. He says, I don't want to be this way Mom, Dad. I don't want to hurt you. I can't believe I did that.

This is what we've been hoping for. God's answered our prayers. The work is done.

But it's not done, by a long shot. He hasn't been transformed yet. Why not? Having a heart broken over sin doesn't in and of itself change the teen's heart. For that, our teen must still go to God and ask Him to create a new heart in him. Until he does that, he remains a brokenhearted rebel, not a transformed rebel.

When we embrace our brokenhearted teen, we put an

arm around him and walk him to the Lord, saying as we go: Come on son, you need heart surgery and I know just where to get it. It's when a teen is brokenhearted that he will be most willing to go along. If we wait, he'll harden. A brokenhearted rebel who tries to be a nice guy is going to fall on his face because there's been no real change of heart. He'll get discouraged and revert to stage two.

That's why we must never take a teen to stage three and leave him there. A brokenhearted teenager must be taught how to talk to Christ, confess his sins, and build a close, personal, relationship with Him.

If our kid has a broken leg and he is in terrible pain, we don't offer him just a hug. We take him to the surgeon, don't we?

It's the same if our kid comes to us with a broken heart, we embrace him and carry him to a spiritual surgeon. That's when real transformation will occur.

Parenting the transformed rebel

A transformed rebel is someone who has opened his heart to Christ and has invited Him to live there and transform it. Once our teen moves to this stage is our job as parents done? Does God take over from here?

No. Even a transformed rebel needs something from his parents.

What does a transformed rebel need? We get help answering this from Paul's letter to the people at Philippi:

Therefore, my dear friends, as you have always obeyed—not only in my presence, but now much more in my absence—continue to work out your salvation with fear and trembling, for it is God who works in you to will and to act according to his good purpose (Phil. 2:12–13).

Three levels of obedience

Notice how Paul makes reference to three different levels of obedience with the phrases, *in my presence*, *in my absence*, and *much more in my absence*. Doing what is expected in the presence of an authority is level one obedience. That's where our children have to start—putting their toys away and making their beds as we watch. If they stay here, though, and don't advance to the higher levels during adolescence, they become nothing more than compliant rebels.

As a person matures, he moves to a second level: doing what is expected in the absence of an authority. This is when parents can come home after being away and say, I gave you some things to do while I was gone, let's see if they're done. Oh, they are. Good!

That's doing what is expected, without supervision. It's a good place for a teenager to be for a while, but we don't want him to stay there. Paul calls the Philippians to a third level of obedience, asking them to do "much more" than is expected.

He is asking them to stretch—to use imagination and creativity, to invent new ways to serve and to love. This is the level at which Patti was operating when she volunteered to speak at her senior retreat. Just as Paul sought to stretch the Philippians, this is what every parent should do for his or her teen when that teen reaches stage three.

There are two ways a parent can do this:

First, by calling attention to our son's or daughter's transformed heart whenever we can catch them in the act of loving. It's the opposite of catching a rebel in the act of sinning, but it's a lot more fun. Whenever we catch our kids in the act of loving, and call it to their attention, it encourages them to stretch even more.

No nap for these kids

On a missions trip with a group of high school students, we left three of the kids behind at the missionary's home for the afternoon. We didn't have space in the van to take them all visiting in the neighborhoods. We left these three with no assigned chores. They could have napped all afternoon if they wanted to.

How do you suppose they decided to spend their time? They got to looking in the kitchen, and found some tarnished pots and pans. They spent all afternoon, without anyone even suggesting it, cleaning the missionary wife's copper pots and pans. When she came home and saw her pots gleaming, she burst into tears. Their thoughtfulness deeply moved her. The kids got caught in the act of loving at level three.

It led to several more spontaneous acts of love during the week.

Second, parents can help their kids at stage three by giving them greater opportunity to operate without supervision. If these kids had been supervised the whole time they would have never had the opportunity to love in their own creative ways. Parents can trust teens at level three with greater freedom because of the change that has begun in their hearts. Without this freedom, they are robbed of the opportunity to learn level three obedience.

God wants voluntary love, not forced love. As we parent our kids at each of the four stages of rebellion, we must never lose sight of this.

Eight

Step One—The Lost Art of Reflection

Earlier in this book, we said one of the biggest mistakes a parent makes is parenting from a position of pressure instead of a position of rest.

In the next four chapters, we're unveiling a fourfold strategy for parenting from rest.

The R in the REST strategy represents the step of Reflection, which we'll develop in this chapter. Reflection is absolutely vital if were going to intervene in a healthy way in our kid's problems. Then, in the three subsequent chapters, we're going to examine Exploration, the second step; Surrender, the third step; and then the creative step of Teaching. When we refer to the REST strategy, we mean:

R   Reflection
E   Exploration
S   Surrender
T   Teaching

Reflection concentrates on us, the parents. Exploration targets the adolescent. Surrender is the step that centers on God. Teaching is the step that considers the problems teens face.

All four are vital if we're going to parent from a position of rest instead of pressure.

Most parents want to jump right to step four. We want to start in teaching without doing the hard work of reflection, exploration, and surrender. This is understandable because it's one of the main responsibilities the Bible gives parents. However, we'll show in this chapter how it is imperative that parents wait to start teaching until they take time to reflect.

Sneaking out to a motel

Theresa told her parents she was spending the night with a girl friend. Technically, this was true. However, instead of spending the night at her friend's house—as the parents believed—the two girls went to a motel, where they were going to spend the night with two college boys. However, Theresa's parents got an anonymous phone call.

"You'd better check on your daughter. She's not where she said she was going to be. Instead of Caroline's house, try looking at Motel 6, room 108."

Ed and Jean quickly acted on the tip. They went to the motel and discovered Theresa exactly where the caller said.

They were shocked at their daughter's deception.

Sixteen-year-old Theresa had never really caused any problems for her parents. She'd been a good girl. But they had caught her in a series of lies over the last two months. It was as if she was leading a double life. Her parents were distraught, almost hysterical. What should they do?

More than anything else, these parents needed to rest—REST. They needed to move systematically through the four steps of the REST strategy. This strategy is designed to guide parents toward a comprehensive biblical response to their kids' problems.

Step 1: Reflection

Let's get into the specifics of reflection and how we do it. Again, let's start with the Bible. The Apostle Paul in his letter to the Christians at Galatia pointed out why reflection must always be part of any strategy to turn rebels around.

> Brothers, if someone is caught in a sin, you who are spiritual should restore him gently. But watch yourself, or you may also be tempted. Carry each other's burdens, and in this way, you will fulfill the law of Christ (Gal. 6:1–2).

The situation Paul described here is exactly what a parent of a troubled teenager faces. Notice the three key verbs in these verses.

The first one is *caught*—"caught up." This describes the spiritual condition almost every teenager finds himself in from time to time—being caught up in behavior that takes him off the track of God's truth.

"Caught up" describes a situation in which the adolescent is unaware of what he's doing. He's not really sure of the significance. He's caught in it almost like a fish caught in a net. The fish can't get out on its own—just like our kids when they find themselves caught up in problem behaviors.

Paul's instructions serve as a guide for parents of troubled teenagers. When someone is caught in a sin—any pattern of behavior that takes him off God's path—Paul states we should *restore* him. This is the second key verb, and it's a medical term. It's a verb that describes the delicate work of restoring or setting a broken bone. Paul clearly said that this kind of spiritual bone-setting must be done gently. It can't be done under pressure, carelessly, or desperately.

The third verb is *watch*, meaning to scope things out. It means to focus on something, to study it, to give it full attention. And Paul said the thing that needs to be watched carefully—if we're going to be active in the process of restoring someone else—is ourselves. When we notice our teen has drifted out of the circle, Paul warned us that we must be careful, as we try to help him, not to veer off the pathway ourselves. A parent can prevent this from happening by watching himself—or by what we'll call in this book, reflection.

C. S. Lewis refers to the process of reflection in *Surprised by Joy* when he writes,

> The surest means of disarming an anger or a lust is to turn your attention from the insult or the girl and start examining the passion itself.
>
> It's easy to storm around, but the quickest way to disarm is to look inside ourselves and ask: "What's going on inside of me that would make me this mad?"

Reflection requires parents to shift their attention from their kids to themselves. Paul warned that failure to do this could result in the parents getting caught up in the same thing as their kids.

When Theresa was dishonest, Ed and Jean were tempted to be dishonest as well. They were tempted to start opening her letters, listening in on her phone calls, telling her that her friends hadn't called when they had. It's tempting when we're trying to help someone else with their rebellion to get caught up in rebellion ourselves. Parents easily get caught up in intimidation, bribery, lying, and a host of other destructive behaviors, in the name of helping our kids. And, of course, we end up hurting them and ourselves instead. This is why, when we're working with our kids to restore them, it's imperative that we watch ourselves even more than we watch them.

The act of watching, which we're calling reflection, is a lost art. It's something not done much today. But it's an art that must be learned if we want to be effective in parenting adolescents. Here's the story of one dad who discovered the value of reflection.

The chess players

One night recently I decided to spend some free time building a happier and closer relationship with my fourteen-year-old daughter. For several weeks she had been urging me to play chess with her, so I suggested a game. She eagerly accepted and we settled down to a most even and challenging match.

It was a school night, however, and at nine o'clock my daughter asked if I could hurry my moves, because she needed to get to bed; she had to get up at six in the morning. I knew her to be rigidly disciplined in her sleeping habits, and it seemed to me that she ought to be able to give up some of this rigidity. I told her:

"Come on, you can go to bed a little later for once. You shouldn't start games that you can't finish. We're having fun."

We played on for another fifteen minutes, during which time she became visibly discomfited. Finally she pleaded "Please, Daddy, please hurry your moves."

I replied, "Chess is a serious game. If you're going to play it well, you're going to play it slowly. If you don't want to play it seriously, you might as well not play it at all."

And so, with her feeling miserable, we continued for another ten minutes, until suddenly my daughter burst into tears, yelled that she conceded the stupid game, and ran weeping up the stairs.

Immediately I felt as if I were nine years old again, lying bleeding in the bushes by the side of the road, next to my bike. Clearly I had made a mistake. Clearly I had failed to negotiate a turn in the road. I had started the evening wanting to have a happy time with my daughter. Ninety minutes later she was in tears and so angry at me she could hardly speak.

What had gone wrong? The answer was obvious. But I did not want to see the answer, so it took me two hours to wade through the pain of accepting the fact that I had botched the evening by allowing my desire to win a chess game become more important than my desire to build a relationship with my daughter. I was depressed in earnest then.

How had I gotten so out of balance? Gradually it dawned on me that my desire to win was too great and that I needed to give up some of this desire. Yet even this little giving up seemed impossible.

All my life my desire to win had served me in good stead, for I had won many things. How was it possible to play chess without wanting to win? I had never been comfortable doing things unenthusiastically. How could I conceivably play chess enthusiastically but not seriously?

Yet somehow I had to change, for I knew that my enthusiasm, my competitiveness, and my seriousness were part of a behavior pattern that was working and would continue to work toward alienating my children from me and that if I were not able to modify this pattern, there would be other times of unnecessary tears and bitterness.*

---

*Peck, *The Road Less Traveled*, 67–68

In the wake of the conflict, this father chose to reflect. Otherwise, he may never have discovered what was really going on between him and his daughter. This is why Jesus told the man with the complaint against his brother to examine his own heart first. Jesus was commanding him to reflect, which is the first step toward transforming our relationships.

Most parents, however, when in the middle of a heated exchange with their teens, don't want to stop and say to themselves: Hey, I better take a look at myself first, before I respond.

Why don't we want to stop and reflect when we're in the midst of an incident like this? Parents give various reasons.

> I don't reflect because I'm afraid of what I might see. I stay busy so I don't have time to stop and think about my life—not even for one minute. I like it better that way.
>
> —Mother of two teens

> Reflect? I don't know how to do that kind of thing. I'm just not built that way. I'm not deep. I tried once to figure out what I do, but I'm no good at it.
>
> —Father of one teen

> I don't stop and look at myself because I wouldn't know what to do with what I found. It's too depressing. I'll just have to depend on God to take care of the inside stuff.
>
> —Father of two teens

Each of these parents is expressing valid concerns—concerns that show us the three biggest reasons why most of us do little reflection. Let's answer the three questions these concerns raise.

Question #1—What will I see if I reflect?

What will I find if I take a close look at myself? This is frightening, for a lot of us know that there's stuff down inside our hearts that we don't want anybody to see, things that we don't want to remember because they're so painful. We each, mistakenly, think that what is in our hearts is unique—that no one else has so many broken, ugly parts, undesirable parts. However, the Bible makes it clear that there are four things that everyone will find if they take time to reflect.

A hungry heart

Every one of us has a hungry heart, no matter where we are in maturity and growth in Christ. Each has a heart that is not fully satisfied and content. In fact, Paul tells us about that hungry heart:

> We know that the whole creation has been groaning as in the pains of childbirth right up to the present time. Not only so, but we ourselves, who have the firstfruits of the Spirit, groan inwardly as we wait eagerly for our adoption as sons, the redemption of our bodies (Rom. 8:22–23).

Groaning is the word Paul uses here to describe the condition of the human heart. And there's nothing like having a teenager in our family to cause our hearts to groan even more.

Theresa's parents reflect

Remember Theresa, the girl who sneaked out to the motel? It didn't take much reflection for her parents to realize they both were approaching the situation in a desperate manner because of their hungry hearts.

Theresa's father, Ed, was losing favor with the top man at his company, so he was feeling unappreciated. He hungered to be valued as a man. He carried that hunger home with him every day, putting pressure on his family to do or say something that would prop up his wilting self-esteem.

Jean, the mom, was also suffering from a hungry heart. She was dying to feel wanted. During her adolescent days, she had been pursued by many boys. That ended when she got married. The need to feel wanted had gotten worse lately. Because Ed was losing the power game at his office, she felt more neglected than ever. She was just dying for a man to show her some attention. When high school boys began showing interest in Theresa, it made Mom "groan" again to have a male pursue her. She wanted to taste it once again.

As Ed and Jean reflected, they both realized they were operating with very hungry hearts. Both knew Christ. Both were Christians, but they were groaning inwardly—Ed, for someone to value him; Jean, for someone to want her.

That's not surprising. Every person who stops and has the courage to reflect is going to find a hunger he or she groans to have satisfied. This hunger has to be watched because a person with an unwatched heart naturally takes desperate measures.

A wicked heart

This is the second quality reflection uncovers. The Bible teaches there is a wicked heart inside each of us.

When Paul was thinking about sending someone to parent the Christians in Philippi, he could only find one person who had the right kind of heart, Timothy.

> I hope in the Lord Jesus to send Timothy to you soon. . . . I have no one else like him, who takes a genuine interest in your welfare. For everyone looks out for his own interests, not those of Jesus Christ (Phil. 2:19–21).

If Paul was looking for someone with a healthy heart to parent our kids, would he pick us? All we have to do is reflect for a short time to start to wonder. We quickly become aware how automatically our hearts look out for no one's interest but our own. That's what makes the human heart wicked.

A deceitful heart

This is the third trait we stub a toe on when we reflect. Our hearts like to hide their real intentions from everyone, even ourselves. Jeremiah 17:9 describes the hearts of human beings as "deceitful above all things." This deceitfulness—left unchecked—pollutes every one of our relationships.

The high school teacher

Stan taught high school math and coached basketball. His three daughters were delightful kids, but lately his oldest, a high school sophomore, was having serious problems with her friends. Every night at supper, Stan would discuss these problems with her. Since he worked with high school students, he fancied himself an expert, of sorts, on teenagers.

The situation had reached near-soap-opera proportions. Nancy's friends were giving her a hard time. They were hurting her and disappointing her. Stan was very concerned about this problem and showed an unusual amount of attention to this every night at supper for nearly a week.

This seventh night was no different. Once again, he talked face-to-face with his daughter throughout almost the whole meal. When supper was over, Nancy went to her room. Stan started to get up, too, when Linda, the middle daughter, who had been listening attentively to the whole conversation, asked to speak with him.

Linda said: "Dad, can I ask you a question?" The father was surprised. He had concentrated so much on Nancy's problems, he'd almost forgotten the rest of the family was at the table.

"I guess so."

"You know, I told you a few weeks ago that I was having some problems with my friends, and you've never asked me about that. Yet, you and Nancy have been talking about her friends every night this week.

"Why do you care about her friends—and not about my friends?"

Stan felt harpooned by his daughter's words. They were piercing. His first impulse was to put the blame for his negligence back on her.

"Linda, you should have reminded me. It's your fault."

But he didn't say this, because Stan knew it wasn't true. He hesitated for a moment, then looked at Linda.

"That's really a good question. I don't know the answer. Let me think about it and get back to you, OK?"

Linda nodded.

"OK, Dad."

Stan spent some time that evening in painful reflection. Why was he over-responsive to one of his daughters' problems and under-responsive to the other?

Suddenly, it became clear. Nancy was in high school, Stan's area of expertise. He prided himself on the way he was able to coach kids both on and off the field. Now that his own daughter was having problems, his reputation was on the line. How could he be seen as an expert if he couldn't solve his own daughter's problems? Linda, however, was a fifth-grader. Her problems offered no threat to his reputation at the high school. Besides, he didn't claim to be an expert on children's problems. That wasn't his area of specialty.

As Stan began to realize what he was doing, he was shocked at the ugliness of his heart. He realized his approach to both his girls was self-serving. But, until now, it had escaped his notice.

As Paul said, everyone looks out for their own interests. No one looks out for the interests of Jesus Christ.

If that's where it stopped for parents, it would be bad enough. But, as in the case of Stan, not only are parents absorbed with their own interests, but most of the time they're oblivious to what those interests truly are.

Those are the consequences of having a deceitful heart.

A fickle heart

That's the fourth characteristic we'll discover when we do some introspection. In the Garden of Gethsemane, the night Jesus was betrayed and arrested, He asked His disciples to stay awake and pray with Him. When He found them fallen asleep, He woke them and said, "Watch and pray!" (Matt. 26:41).

He wasn't asking them to watch out for the mob, or for the Roman soldiers, or even for Judas, who was about to betray Him. He was asking them to watch out for themselves. Why did Jesus warn them, "Watch and pray so you will not fall into temptation"? He knew that the human heart is fickle.

Hosea observed the same thing, when he said of the Israelites: "Your love is like the morning mist, like the early dew that disappears" (Hos. 6:4).

Our hearts tend to wander. Unwatched hearts wander off the pathway of God's truth. Like Stan with his daughters, a parent's heart without reflection will creep unnoticed back into self-serving patterns of parenting.

This is the consequence of having a fickle heart.

Question #2—How can I see what's in my own heart?

We know the human heart is wicked, hungry, deceptive, and fickle. We know if we reflect very long we'll see evidence of all four traits in our hearts. But how do we go about reflecting on our own hearts? Just as we use mirrors to see what's on our faces, we also have to use mirrors to see what's in our hearts. God provides three mirrors for us to do this very thing. Of course, no mirror tells the whole story, but the three together can give an honest seeker accurate insight into his own inner workings.

The mirror of intimate relationships

Although this mirror isn't a hundred percent accurate, it gives us a picture of ourselves the way those most intimately involved with us see us.

When fifth-grade Linda asked Stan why he was interested in Nancy's problems, but not hers, that was a mirror for him. Linda was giving her dad a glimpse into what was in his own heart.

Our kids' feedback is not always reliable. Sometimes kids make things up, distort, exaggerate things to manipulate us, to make us feel bad, to get us to give in. However, on those occasions when they speak to us from their hearts, telling us their honest feelings, they can be a rich source of information about ourselves. Of course, so can our spouses, parents, and friends.

The great Old Testament figure King David completely ignored just such a mirror provided him by his wife, Michal. She held up a mirror to his behavior and said she didn't like what she had seen of his actions in the streets that day (2 Sam. 6:16–23).

David resented that and distanced himself from Michal for the rest of his life, to avoid ever looking into that mirror again. This was a serious mistake. Had David used the mirror God was providing through Michal, he would have been far less vulnerable to temptation by Bathsheba a short time later. Reflection was a powerful tool that David used on many occasions. This time, however, he neglected to reflect but let his heart continue to operate on auto pilot.

Remember what an unwatched heart does? It wanders off the track of God's truth. That's what happened to David.

How can we avoid the mistake David made? We need to give the people around us, especially those closest to us, permission to be honest with us, then take the feedback they give us and honestly weigh it as Stan weighed his fifth-grader's feedback. In this way, our intimate relationships can provide us with one of our most accurate mirrors.

The mirror of God's people

Consider this verse:

> See to it, brothers, that none of you has a sinful, unbelieving heart that turns away from the living God. But encourage one another daily, as long as it is called Today, so that none of you may be hardened by sin's deceitfulness (Heb. 3:12–13).

The writer of Hebrews says we should encourage one another, talk to one another, to keep us from becoming hardened by the deceitfulness of our own hearts. In this way, God's people can be a mirror to us.

> Like a coating of glaze over earthenware
>> are fervent lips with an evil heart.
> A malicious man disguises himself with his lips,
>> but in his heart he harbors deceit.
> Though his speech is charming, do not believe him,
>> for seven abominations fill his heart.
> His malice may be concealed by deception,
>> but his wickedness will be exposed in the assembly (Prov. 26:23–26).

The first several times we read these verses we probably don't think of them as describing us. But the longer we live and the more we enter into the process of reflection, the more we see ourselves in this passage. We can fake it with our words but still harbor deceit in our hearts. That's why everyone of us ought to have some group of God's people (an "assembly") that we get together with on a regular basis. And this group should have our permission to give us feedback—to tell us how we're doing.

The mirror of God's Word

This third mirror is certainly the most reliable. Without God's Word, it will be very difficult to get an accurate glimpse of ourselves. The Bible is like a spotlight that shines in our lives and illumines the darkest and most remote recesses of our hearts. Remember what James said:

> Anyone who listens to the word but does not do what it says is like a man who looks at his face in a mirror and, after looking at himself, goes away and immediately forgets what he looks like (James 1:23–24).

The Bible is like a pair of eyeglasses. Without it, we are spiritually far-sighted. We won't be able to see ourselves accurately—even in the other mirrors of intimate relationships and of the people of God.

I got up one morning, dressed, and ate breakfast. When I got in the car, I stuck my glasses on my face, then drove to work. When I got out of the car, I noticed I was wearing shoes that didn't match!

With my glasses on, it was so clear. There they were—a brown shoe with a tassel and a black shoe with laces! There was no way they looked alike. Somehow, though, back at the house without my glasses on, I'd figured they matched.

That's what it's like trying to know ourselves without looking at our reflection in the mirror of God's Word. Throughout this book we've been holding up the Bible and using it as a mirror for parents. Looking at ourselves in it is often uncomfortable or downright agonizing. But according to James, if we fail to do this we'll quickly forget what kind of people we are—what kind of things have to be dealt with in our hearts.

Question #3—What do I do with what I find in my heart?

Mirrors give us the tools to reflect. Reflection exposes our broken hearts. The question remains, what do we do with our broken hearts once they're exposed?

That was the challenge facing Ed and Jean, whose daughter sneaked off to the motel. They knew Theresa needed help. That was obvious. But what about themselves? Reflection revealed their condition, their wicked hearts. They were hostile toward Theresa. They wanted her to quit disrupting their lives. Their hearts had to be dealt with before they could approach Theresa with hearts at rest. It was time for Ed and Jean to bring themselves to God as brokenhearted rebels. This was a stage they had to come to before they would be capable of guiding their daughter to it.

In the preceding chapter we observed in Hosea 14:1–3 that the process of transformation begins with putting our spiritual needs into words.

Put it into words

This happened for Ed and Jean in a small support group of parents in their church. It was in this group they got the help they needed to reflect. One evening, they put their own needs into words for the first time.

Ed: I'm hungry for somebody to listen to me when I talk. I want to be important to somebody.

That was a first for him. It had been inside, eating away at him for years.

Jean: When I see Theresa with those guys, and they're calling her and coming over, my heart just aches. I want to be wanted like she is. I know what that used to feel like and I want to feel it again. I'm so hungry to feel wanted. I guess the way I'm trying to feel wanted is to make Theresa very popular. If she's wanted by a lot of her male friends, then I'll be wanted. I've given up on Ed. He's so preoccupied and in so much pain with his own hungers, I've realized I'm never going to feel it from him.

This turned the lights on for Jean. Putting it into words made the problem crystal clear to her.

When we do this like Ed and Jean did, we must make sure the words we pick attach the proper seriousness to the matter. The Old Testament prophet Jeremiah challenged the Israelites to get serious about their own hearts.

> From the least to the greatest,
>   all are greedy for gain;
> prophets and priests alike,
>   all practice deceit.
> They dress the wound of my people
>   as though it were not serious.
> "Peace, peace," they say,
>   when there is no peace (Jer. 6:13–14).

Jeremiah warned his listener not to treat a serious wound as if it needed nothing more than a Band-aid. He would warn parents like Ed and Jean not to ask God for an aspirin tablet if what they need is heart surgery: *God, I just have this small problem—I want to strangle my daughter. It's just a small problem that I figure two spiritual headache pills will take care of.*

Instead, Jeremiah urges us to use words that accurately reflect the seriousness of the matter: *God, I've got cancer— spiritual cancer. I'm going to destroy my daughter if I keep playing emotional games with her that are directed at pump-*

ing up my own self-esteem. I'm jealous of my daughter. I'm into power games with her. I want my ego massaged.

Our words should reflect the nature of the wickedness, the extent of it, and our helplessness in dealing with it: God, I can't rip this thing out myself. I can't. It's too much for me.

The final step is to take these words and pour them out to God, asking Him to give us the one thing we need most as parents, but could never attain without Him.

Freedom!

We need freedom from our wicked hearts. Look what God says He'll do when we take our broken hearts to Him.

I will heal their waywardness
> and love them freely,
>> for my anger has turned away from them.
I will be like the dew to Israel;
> he will blossom like a lily.
Like a cedar of Lebanon
> he will send down his roots;
>> his young shoots will grow (Hos. 14:4–6).

Don't miss the promise in the last phrase: our young shoots will grow.

This is the growth in our teenagers that only God's Spirit can cause. We provide the fertile ground for this to happen in our homes when we practice the lost art of reflection.

Nine

Step Two—Exploration Improves Understanding

Shelly was a sophomore in high school when she began to insist that her family do more to honor the Sabbath. This girl in the past had enjoyed such Sunday activities as going out with the youth group for pizza, playing games, tennis. Suddenly she came to the conclusion that it was wrong to do anything on Sundays but worship the Lord and think about Him. She told her parents that it was a sin for them to go out to eat at a restaurant after church on Sunday.

She also criticized them for buying gas on Sunday.

"It requires people to work on the Sabbath," she said.

In addition, Shelly started to starve herself all week long "for spiritual purposes." As her reason, she quoted several Bible passages advocating fasting.

She began to lose weight and become sickly. When her parents pressured her to eat, she claimed that they were trying to get her to disobey the Lord.

Worried about her sickly appearance and zealous behavior, they didn't know what to do. Anything they did to discourage it was perceived by Shelly as an attempt to hurt her relationship with the Lord. She was succeeding in making them wonder if the problem was their own lack of spirituality.

What do you think? Were Shelly's actions coming out of a heart that was unusually close to Christ?

Or did Shelly have a heart that was rebellious to Christ? The only way we can know is to explore the pressures behind Shelly's behavior.

Exploration—the second step of the REST strategy—involves studying our adolescent to discover what kinds of pressures are acting on her. To explore means to find out what kinds of pressures might be at work in her life to persuade her to move off God's pathway of truth.

It's important to be aware that our teens are constantly being pushed by their world to go in one direction or the other. All problem behavior in adolescence has a "push" behind it.

Kids don't choose their behaviors randomly. They don't act the way they do because they're weird. One comedian in his stand-up routine says, half-kiddingly and half-seriously, that kids behave the way they do because they're "brain damaged." That's why there is no logical reason for their behavioral choices.

It's a funny routine. However, it's not true. The truth of the matter is that teens are very logical in their choices of behavior. Most of the time we just haven't taken the time to understand what their logic is.

What is pushing, motivating, or persuading them to choose certain behaviors? These pressures give us understanding of where the behavior comes from.

Where was Shelly's behavior going? What was its logical goal? Why did it pop up now, in the middle of her sophomore year? Were Shelly's actions a result of forced love or voluntary love? Was there real evidence of a love for God and people underneath it? Or was there something else behind it?

These are the types of questions we ask when we explore. The first step of the REST strategy, reflection, focuses on understanding what is behind our actions as parents. The second step, exploration, focuses on what's behind our teen's actions.

Two types of pressures

As we begin to explore our teen's life, we must have some idea of what we're looking for. Look for two broad kinds of pressures—internal and external.

To find the external pressures that affect our teen's behavior, study her world. That's a foreign place for most parents. There's no way most of us understand what it's like to live in her world, sit at her desk, hang out with her friends.

To find the internal pressures, we must study her behavior—what it accomplishes for her, what it gains for her personally. We know every teen is hungry to experience certain things. In fact she's been built by God to experience these things. These unsatisfied hungers fuel her actions and give her direction. If we understand how she benefits from these behaviors, we will know the internal hunger that pressures her to behave this way.

In Shelly's case, what would motivate a sophomore to fast, to starve herself? What would drive her? Where would the power come from to face that kind of pain? Psalm 8 will not only help us understand what drives Shelly, but also what drives every adolescent.

> What is man that you are mindful of him,
>> the son of man that you care for him?
> You made him a little lower than the heavenly beings
>> and crowned him with glory and honor.
>
> You made him ruler over the works of your hands;
>> you put everything under his feet (Psalm 8:4–6).

In these verses, David reflects on three lofty things God created every human being to experience. They're not small things at all. They're huge. It's built into every human being's nature to desire these things and to hunger for them when they're not present. Adolescents desire them as much as adults, and often there's nowhere in a teenager's world she can go to enjoy them.

Internal pressure

Let's call the first one **warmth**. Humans were created to experience a warm, caring relationship with God: to know that He is mindful of them, that He thinks about them, that He's attentive to them and to their needs. Teens were created to experience this kind of warmth.

Call the second one **height**. God says human beings are the highest form of creation in His universe besides angels. He honors us, values us, and gives us glory. He's created us to be crowned. A crown rests on top. It makes us higher than anything else.

God built human beings to experience a third thing as well. He built us to experience power or authority over our world, to command our world to do certain things—and the world obey. Can you imagine the power of going out into our yards, looking at our grass, and saying:

"OK, now, that's high enough, grass!"

And the grass says, "OK."

Or commanding mosquitoes to stay away from us while we're having a picnic lunch. And they obey!

Human beings were created to have that kind of power over our world. Let's call it **weight**. Have you ever caught yourself wishing you had some weight to throw around some power, some influence? We were created to have weight.

Three things: warmth, height, weight. We were created to experience them all. And, because our kids have been created in the same image, they also hunger to experience these things in their world—maybe even more than adults do, since they are more experience-oriented than goal-oriented. They don't have the ability adults do to postpone experiencing these until certain goals are achieved. Our kids don't want to wait. Whatever experience in the here and now that offers the most warmth, height, and weight usually is what our kids go after. This is what pressures a teenager from the inside to behave the way she does.

Warmth. Kids who are overweight are usually hungering for warmth. They want so much to be cared for and to be nurtured. They can experience that for a few seconds or minutes when they're eating, bingeing. But as soon as the food's gone, the warmth is gone. They eat constantly because as long as they are eating, there is a sense of warmth. We feel warm when someone—or something—is attending, caring, nurturing, being mindful of us. If warmth isn't being provided, our kids will have an unsatisfied hunger that will pressure them to move in whatever direction will provide warmth.

Height. How do kids find height? Remember when we were growing up we couldn't wait to get to the next grade? In grade school, we all wanted to be sixth graders. Why? So we'd be the biggest kids in the school—the most valued.

When kids get to junior high school, they feel small, or short, again. They're no longer a cut above, just regular, average kids belonging to that huge group called a student body. So where will they get their sense of height? How will they feel special? By being "taller" in someone's eyes than other people. That's when they choose to do things, sometimes in desperation, that will make them look tall in the eyes of their friends—talk big, act big, dress big. To achieve height, they'll go to any lengths they must.

Weight. Where do our kids go to experience power, or weight? They're looking for something that can be under them, something that they can put their feet on. Remember

Psalm 8 said that humans were created to have all creation under our feet? Well, most of the time, kids feel just the opposite, like everybody's got their feet on them.

What teens are dying for is to be able to dominate in some way—to feel the weight of having something under their control. That's why older siblings will boss younger ones. It helps them feel some weight, some power. That's why positions of power at school are pursued. Kids want to feel some kind of power. They want to feel weight. When nothing's giving them this, they will be driven by this unsatisfied hunger.

Seldom do our kids experience the satisfaction of all three needs at the same time. Usually they have to settle for one at the expense of the other two.

For example, a lot of kids, in their desire to feel power, think they have to be obnoxious or to break the rules. They disturb a class and get the teacher flustered, make her forget where she is in her notes, maybe even get her to lose her temper. What does that prove? The teenager now feels she is weightier than the teacher. She's got clout. She can mess up the whole class.

In order to get weight, though, what did she lose? She lost warmth. Most people don't want to be friends with a troublemaker. And, she lost height, because no one will call her up during an awards assembly and give her a plaque for being disruptive in class.

As she sacrifices warmth and height to feel weight, she comes to depend more and more on her disruptive behavior as her only source of nourishment.

This is similar to what was going on in Shelly's life, the high school girl who was making a big deal about the Sabbath.

Shelly got warmth from her mother, who waited on her constantly, nurturing her as if she were still a small child. She experienced some degree of height at church where she was regarded as the most spiritual kid in the youth group. As such, however, she felt constrained to live up to everyone's expectations. She felt little freedom to be her own person. Both the environment at home and at church made her feel powerless. She hungered to feel strong.

For the first time, Shelly was able to experience a semblance of weight (power) by interrupting her family's plans to go out to Sunday dinner. She said to herself, Can you believe that I could be that powerful? She found a way to be a rebel without blowing her cover as the most spiritual kid at church. She could completely baffle and control her parents with words like, "Oh no. It's the Lord's will that I don't eat. I have made a vow to Him. I'm going to fast."

All of a sudden, Shelly was in charge. She was more powerful than her parents. The one thing that she was hungering for, weight, she could now enjoy. But she was enjoying it at her family's expense. This was the internal pressure driving Shelly. Internal pressures, however, are only half the story when we're trying to understand our adolescent. There are also external pressures.

External pressures

To discover a kid's greatest external pressures we must explore her most important relationships. Every teen is pressured to do whatever she must to make her relationships more nourishing. If she is starving to feel warmth, she will do whatever she has to get others to be warm towards her, even if she has to get off the track of God's truth.

The graph below shows how an adolescent's primary relationships change between the ages of ten and twenty-two.

It's in preadolescence that a child's relationship with her parents begins to change. Although she still gets the bulk of her warmth, height, and weight from them, she's starting to get more and more from her friends.

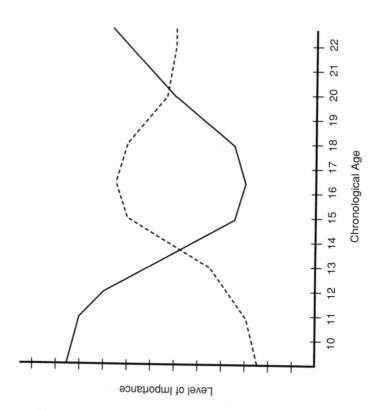

How an Adolescent's Relationships Change

As she enters adolescence, her relationships with her friends become more important than her relationships with her parents. She starts to get the bulk of her nourishment from her friends. Sometime between the ages of fourteen and seventeen, her closeness to her parents hits an all-time low. It is not until late adolescence that her relationships with her parents begin to regain their importance. They probably will never regain the level they had when she was a child, but they do return to a level of great significance.

What can we conclude by looking at this? Obviously, during adolescence, our kids will feel a lot of pressure from their friends. They will look a lot less to us to have their need met for warmth, height, and weight.

When she was smaller, we used to hold our kid, rock her, kiss her. That gave her warmth. However, this gets awkward when she becomes an adolescent. It's not as awkward for her to turn to a friend for warmth. Now she can get the holding, rocking, and kissing from a boyfriend. Imagine how the parents feel when they observe their daughter turning to someone else to get her needs met. Suddenly, they feel guilty, scared, and angry—all at the same time.

Much to their daughter's consternation, they begin putting limitations on how often she can be with this boy. Now, instead of a source of warmth, the girl perceives her parents to be a source of frustration.

She thinks, I can't believe how cruel you're being. Don't you know I was created to feel cared about, to feel warm and nurtured. He's the only one who can give warmth to me and you're trying to stop it. I hate you for that.

She feels justified to be rebellious, to sneak out at night, or to lie and to see him when she's not supposed to.

Before her parents go any farther, it's imperative they understand the pressure behind their daughter's actions. It's like conducting a diagnostic exam on our adolescent, much as a doctor would on his or her patient before prescribing medicine.

Doctors don't write prescriptions unless they've done an examination and have a clear idea of what they're dealing with. Symptoms for one illness can resemble those of another illness, and the wrong medicine could make the illness worse instead of better.

Like doctors, when we see problem behavior in our adolescent we must stop to do an examination before we respond. Or else we could respond in a way that only makes the problem worse.

Bad grades for three kids

To illustrate this, let's take three adolescents whose grades have recently dropped.

The first one is Larry. Larry is hungry for warmth. His parents are preoccupied and busy most of the time. Both work outside the home. Both are pursuing their own careers. Both are excited about their own lives. They're very busy on weekends. They've got a lot of toys—boats, skis, sports cars. So they're not around for this kid who is starving for some sense of warmth.

This is the external pressure of parental neglect. Larry's parents aren't even aware of how little nourishment they are providing in their relationship with him. They just figure, Larry's busy, just like us. He's got a lot of friends. He's running around a lot. He doesn't seem to be sitting around. He doesn't really need us. They feel free to concentrate on their world and let Larry alone.

When they finally find out about their son's bad grades, they decide to get involved.

They decide to stay home more. They decide to have supper every night as a family. And after supper they make sure he works on his homework.

Although their response seems good on the surface, it fails to take into account what Larry was trying to accomplish with his under achievement. He was trying to get his mom and dad to give him some warmth. What have these parents done in responding to the low grades in the way they have? They've reinforced Larry's under achievement.

What chances are there now that this kid will intentionally work on his grades and get them back up? Very little, because he's discovered the only way he can get his parents to pay attention to him is by underachieving. Why should he try harder? He would be giving up the only behavior that has been successful in creating warmth for him.

A's didn't work, so—

Sharon has the same problem. But her grades are bad for a different reason. This girl is hungry for weight. She wants to feel like she has some power, some control, some influence.

Her parents are around all the time, but nothing is ever good enough for them. They always demand more. They make her feel as if she can't do anything right. Her last report card was all A's—but one. Sharon's parents pointed at the one grade and asked, "What about this B? You'd better pick up the pace, because in college the teachers will be harder."

When she expresses her opinions to them, she feels belittled. "What do you know about the economy?" they ask.

Finally, she lets her grades drop as a way of expressing her anger and distress. Of course, her parents become enraged. They start to argue with one another about whose fault this is. Their nice, ordered world is thrown into turmoil.

For the first time, Sharon starts to feel weight. She was powerful enough to get her parents upset. They're yelling and screaming. They're not sleeping well. They're fighting with each other about her. They're so upset they change their plans for the weekend.

That's power! Now, who has the weight around the house? Sharon's discovered she has the power to take away her parents' joy. She may not be powerful enough to capture their praise, but she's powerful enough to get their goat. By responding the way they did, her parents have reinforced the problem behavior.

Still another reason for bad grades

Let's take one more kid who also has bad grades. This time it's Jason—who is hungry for height. But wait a minute! That doesn't make sense. If he's hungry for recognition he should want to be a cut above, to stand above his classmates. Wouldn't that translate into a desire for a high class ranking, better grade point averages? That way he would be taller than everybody else. Why would someone who is hungry for height choose to let his grades drop? The behavior is logical as soon as you understand the internal and external pressures on Jason.

In this case, the external pressure again comes from his parents, who are constantly protecting him. They won't let him try much on his own. They're afraid he'll fail, get hurt, get tired, or get sick.

Recently, he decided he wanted to take some tougher courses. His parents said, No, you better not. You really have to be careful. You have that medical condition. We don't want you having any more seizures.

Every time Jason chooses to do something that will enable him to stand out, his parents won't permit it. After a while, he gives up, becomes depressed, and quits trying. Naturally, his grades drop. After seeing these grades, his parents say, This proves our kid is fragile. He can't take the responsibility other kids can handle. We'll have to home school him since he can't keep up with the other kids."

What have these parents just done? They've just reinforced the problem behavior. By putting the possibility of height among his peers even farther out of his reach, they've intensified his helplessness and despair.

Every kid is different, even though her problem behavior may seem similar to someone else's. Therefore, parents must explore before we respond. We must explore what's going on in her most important relationships and what's going on in her heart. The first reason we should explore before we respond to problem behavior is that if we don't, in all probability we will only reinforce it.

There's a second reason why we should explore before we respond.

If we don't explore, we will have difficulty feeling any compassion for her when she rebels. Remember, no rebellion occurs in a vacuum. The vilest criminal commits crimes as a result of a hungry heart and a hostile world. When we take time to explore the pressures behind unhealthy behavior, we start to feel compassion for the individual. This is a prerequisite for parenting an adolescent rebel.

When a kid's grades start to drop, wise parents sit down and explore what's going on. Is she starving for warmth? That's no sin. On the contrary, she was created by God to experience warmth, but lives in a world that withholds it. When parents start to understand this, they begin to have the same kind of compassion for their child that Christ did when He saw the crowds and had compassion on them because they were *harassed* and *helpless*. "Harassed" speaks of external pressure; "helpless" speaks of internal pressure.

When Jesus was out among the masses, no matter how rebellious they were, He saw the pressures on them and was moved with compassion. Instead of writing them off, He said, Let's pray that God will send them shepherds (see Matt. 9:38).

When parents have this kind of compassion for their kids, their main concern becomes, how can I shepherd this kid back into relationship with Christ?

Exploration gives parents the data they need to make a relationship with Christ relevant and attractive to their kids. Through exploration parents discover what the teen is hungry for. Through teaching, the fourth step in the REST strategy, parents show how to find it in Christ.

However, when we explore what's going on with our kids, we start to realize that their problems are bigger than we are. Any illusion that we can fix them ourselves is shattered. There's nothing left to do but surrender—surrender them to Christ, third step of the REST strategy. Although this seems like a scary place to be, it's a really good place to be. It leads to rest. This is why exploration and the development of exploratory skills is so important for parents.

The three most important exploratory skills are observation, listening, and questioning. Observation requires the use of the eyes; listening, the ears; questioning, the tongue.

Observation

Observation requires getting to a place where we can watch our kids in unguarded moments—especially when we can see them interacting with their friends.

A few years ago I had an unexpected opportunity to observe my junior high daughter. She asked me if she could go to a concert; I said yes—not realizing until it was too late that I was going to have to wait in line with her all night to buy the tickets. There we were—me, my daughter, and about ten million junior high girls—camping out on the sidewalk. And to make matters worse, it rained all night. What an opportunity to observe junior high girls in unguarded moments with their peers! I certainly learned a lot about how they operate, how they talk, how they think.

If we're going to observe and develop that exploratory ability we have to get in places where we can observe our kids during unguarded moments, in their world, dealing with their pressures.

Listening

Listening requires meeting our kids in places where they feel comfortable to talk.

Adolescents tend to talk the best when they're in casual settings, participating in activities they enjoy. When parents share these kinds of activities with the kids, it becomes a safe environment for them to begin to open up. And the more kids talk, the more parents will understand about the pressures they feel.

Questioning

Questioning may be the most important exploratory skill of all. There are three types of questions that parents can ask: investigative, interrogative, and exploratory. Parents tend to be much more skilled at using the first two types.

Investigative questions

Doctors are good at investigative questions. Their purpose is to get information. Investigative questions might include:

- Where are you going?
- Who's taking you?
- What are you going to do when you get there?
- When are you getting home?

These questions are not necessarily adversarial, but neither do they reflect a desire for more involvement on the part of the investigator.

Interrogative questions

The purpose of interrogative questions is to uncover what a person might be hiding. Police officers use them a lot. Parents sound like cops when they say:

- Tell me what you're hiding.
- What did you do tonight?

- Where did you go?
- What did you say?
- Do you have your homework done?
- Did you do all of it?
- Did you do the stuff I told you to do?

Of course these kinds of questions make kids defensive. They feel like they're being set up to be punished. So they close up and hide more.

Exploratory questions

These kinds of questions say a lot to kids. They say, I'd love to know you:

- How did it go today?
- What's happening with your friendship with John?
- What are you feeling about your psychology class?
- How are you feeling about college these days?
- What's going through your mind?

They're questions that invite kids to explain. They're questions that communicate involvement and personal concern by the explorer. They're the only kind of questions that will be successful in motivating an adolescent to talk about what's in her heart.

These exploratory skills that have been briefly described can only be developed through practice. Sometimes it's better to practice using them with other adults before you try them on your kids. Parent support groups are a great environment for honing exploratory skills.

Exploration is an integral part of the REST strategy. The more we explore the pressures that drive our kids, the sooner we'll be ready to surrender them.

Ten

Step Three—Surrendering Your Teens to God's Love

We've spent our entire lives preparing for the step of surrender.

At each stage of our kid's growth and development, we've been asked to surrender her—in a new way.

The first time we took her to the church nursery, at the door we were asked to surrender our child to the care of the nursery worker.

That's hard for every set of parents. Remember those first few weeks, how we took turns standing just outside the auditorium door, holding our little baby girl because we didn't want to surrender her yet?

Then there was the first night she had a baby-sitter. The dinner was unimportant as we kept coming up with reasons to call home.

Of course, the worst was that first day at preschool, when we dropped her off for a whole morning!

Agonized is the best way to describe how we felt when we surrendered her to hospital nurses and doctors as they wheeled her into surgery.

At every stage of our child's development, we're called upon to surrender her to someone else's care. It is perhaps the most difficult thing we'll ever be required to do.

Why is surrender so hard for parents? Paul put his finger on it when he wrote, as a parent might, in 1 Thessalonians 2:17–3:5,

> But, brothers, when we were torn away from you for a short time (in person, not in thought), out of our intense longing we made every effort to see you. For we wanted to come to you—certainly, I, Paul, did, again and again—but Satan stopped us. For what is our hope, our joy, or the crown in which we will glory in the presence of our Lord Jesus when he comes? Is it not you? Indeed, you are our glory and joy.
>
> So when we could stand it no longer, we thought it best to be left by ourselves in Athens. We sent Timothy, who is our brother and God's fellow worker in spreading the gospel of Christ, to strengthen and encourage you in your faith, so that no one would be unsettled by these trials. . . . For this reason, when I could stand it no longer, I sent to find out about your faith. I was afraid that in some way the tempter might have tempted you and our efforts might have been useless.

Paul felt as a dad might who just dropped his daughter off at the college dormitory and drove home.

The Thessalonians were his "glory" and his "joy."

He gloried in his kids' growth, in their development, and in their successes. They were his joy. That made it tough to surrender them and admit he really didn't have control over what would happen to them.

Paul expressed the emotions all parents feel.

He was afraid his efforts to parent them to maturity might fail. All parents fear that something's going to happen to abort the good things they've been trying to accomplish in their kids' lives. They worry that bad influences or bad companions are going to get hold of them and ruin them.

When our kids head out into the world making their own choices, it becomes more and more difficult to surrender them. The less we can control circumstances that are important to us, the more we fear. Our fears grow as our control over our kids diminishes. From the crib to elementary school, from junior high to high school, our kids grow more and more independent of us, leaving us with less and less control.

Just as with Paul, this loss of control stirs up strong feelings and forces within us. These feelings seem to peak during adolescence—especially when a problem hits. Let's look at the chain of turmoil that takes place in a parent's heart during this time.

Loss of control produces fear

Fear says: We are going to lose our daughter. Many different events can balloon the fears we have about our kids and send anxiety shooting through our bodies. Every parent feels it differently. For some, it's a tightening in the chest. For others, it's a dry throat. Others begin to perspire. Some get headaches. It's as if our brains are sending messages to our bodies shouting, Do something now!

Fear generates pressure

Pressure says: I have to do something. Fear sends our minds running in a hundred different directions at once—looking for a solution.

Maybe I'll send her to a Christian college where they've got rules . . . dorm parents . . . chapel . . . Or maybe I'll take her to a counselor . . . or maybe I can . . .

This pressure doesn't let up until the threat of harm to our kids is removed and the fear subsides. But worst of all, the pressure clouds our thinking and affects our judgment. This is the worst time to make decisions because nothing seems clear.

Pressure gives rise to confusion

Confusion says: What should I do? The pressure we feel to do something to help our kids demands immediate action. It tells us to do whatever it takes to get the situation under control now. But it doesn't tell us what to do. Who knows what it will take?

Maybe somebody else's had a similar experience . . . I'll go down to the bookstore and pick up the fifteen books on adolescence . . . Or I'll listen to the radio program . . . Somewhere there must be someone who can tell me the right thing to do.

Finally, just to escape the confusion, we try something.

Confusion leads to desperation

Desperation says: Doing anything is better than nothing! A desperate parent doesn't have time to develop a strategy. He or she just acts—the opposite of Paul's declaration in 1 Corinthians 9:26, "I do not run like a man running aimlessly; I do not fight like a man beating the air."

Desperate parents run aimlessly and beat the air. They're driven by fear, pressure, and confusion. More often than not, their decisions are destructive and end up making matters worse for their kids.

What can parents do to interrupt this chain of turmoil? We can't stop feeling fear for our children when something is threatening them. Paul couldn't—as mature as he was. And what parent can avoid feeling the pressure to do something when his or her kid is in trouble?

And when the situations facing adolescents are often so complex that not even the experts agree about what should be done, how can parents escape confusion?

The chain cannot be broken at the points of fear, of pressure, or of confusion. It's at the point of desperation that parents have the opportunity to escape. Parenting adolescents often requires desperate measures. But desperate behavior is not the only choice. We have two options.

Option #1—Desperate behavior

Steve chose desperate behavior. He had tried every possible way to get his teenage daughter to quit her defiant behaviors: drinking, sexual activity, refusing to come home at curfew.

He felt he had tried everything, but without success. Finally, one night he just hauled off and hit her, sending her flying across the room. In the pandemonium that followed this incident, Steve was asked why he hit his daughter. His answer: I had no choice. I had to do something.

There may be some truth to the second part of the statement. Steve had to do something. But it isn't true that he had no choices. Even a desperate parent has choices. Steve chose desperate behavior.

Desperate behavior in parents takes on many forms. For Steve, it took on the form of verbal intimidation and physical fighting. This is the same desperate measure that Nehemiah resorted to when he got fed up with the Israelites he was trying to parent.

> Moreover, in those days I saw men of Judah who had married women from Ashdod, Ammon, and Moab. Half of their children spoke the language of Ashdod or the language of one of the other peoples, and did not know how to speak the language of Judah. I rebuked them and called curses down on them. I beat some of the men and pulled out their hair. I made them take an oath in

God's name and said: "You are not to give your
daughters in marriage to their sons, nor are you to
take their daughters in marriage for your sons or
for yourselves. Was it not because of marriages
like these that Solomon king of Israel sinned?
Among the many nations there was no king like
him. He was loved by his God, and God made him
king over all Israel, but even he was led into sin by
foreign women. Must we hear now that you too
are doing this terrible wickedness and are being
unfaithful to our God by marrying foreign
women?"

One of the sons of Joiada son of Eliashib the
high priest was son-in-law to Sanballat the Horon-
ite. And I drove him away from me (Neh. 13:23–
29).

If this wasn't such a serious situation, this scene would
almost be comedic. But Nehemiah's actions were tragic. It
was the first time in his strong, patient ministry he resorted to
desperate behavior with the Israelites. At best, it accomplished temporary compliance, but not the change of heart he
longed for. Desperate behavior never does.

Another form of desperate behavior is bargaining. Samson's parents bargained with him when he got off the pathway
of God's truth over this same issue of marrying an unbeliev-
ing woman. In Christian circles, we often see parents entering
into silent conspiracies with their teenagers just as Samson's
parents did: We'll let you go outside God's moral boundaries
in some quiet, subtle ways if you promise not to embarrass us
publicly. Just don't show us up at church.

That's bargaining. It's buying kids off.

Calling in the Assyrians is another type of desperate
behavior. This was a strategy commonly used by the Israelites.

When Ephraim saw his sickness, and Judah his
sores, then Ephraim turned to Assyria, and sent to
the great king for help. But he is not able to cure
you, not able to heal your sores (Hos. 5:13).

Likewise, parents today are often quick at "calling in the
Assyrians" to cure their rebellious adolescents. Too many parents believe that educators and psychologists have the ultimate solutions for their kids, and they turn to them like the
Israelites turned to Assyria.

Running away is another desperate parental behavior.
David tried to run away from his kids when they started
exhibiting problems. He distanced himself emotionally and
physically from them as long as he could. It backfired, however, just like all the other forms of desperate behaviors are
destined to do.

Parents have another way to go, though. Desperate
behavior is not the only recourse when we find ourselves
overwhelmed with fear, pressure, confusion.

Option #2—Desperate prayer

Ezra models this option for us in circumstances very
similar to those in which Nehemiah resorted to desperate
behavior. Notice how different the results are when a parent
resorts to desperate prayer.

After these things had been done, the leaders
came to me and said, "The people of Israel, including the priests and the Levites, have not kept themselves separate from the neighboring peoples with
their detestable practices, like those of the Canaan-
ites, Hittites, Perizzites, Jebusites, Ammonites,
Moabites, Egyptians and Amorites. They have
taken some of their daughters as wives for them-

selves and their sons, and have mingled the holy race with the peoples around them. And the leaders and officials have led the way in this unfaithfulness."

When I heard this, I tore my tunic and cloak, pulled hair from my head and beard and sat down appalled. Then everyone who trembled at the words of the God of Israel gathered around me because of this unfaithfulness of the exiles. And I sat there appalled until the evening sacrifice.

Then, at the evening sacrifice, I rose from my self-abasement, with my tunic and cloak torn, and fell on my knees with my hands spread out to the LORD my God and prayed. . . .

While Ezra was praying and confessing, weeping and throwing himself down before the house of God, a large crowd of Israelites—men, women, and children—gathered around him. They too wept bitterly. Then Schecaniah son of Jehiel, one of the descendants of Elam, said to Ezra, "We have been unfaithful to our God by marrying foreign women from the peoples around us. But in spite of this, there is still hope for Israel. Now let us make a covenant before our God to send away all these women and their children, in accordance with the counsel of my lord and of those who fear the commands of our God. Let it be done according to the Law. Rise up; this matter is in your hands. We will support you, so take courage and do it (Ezra 9:1–6; 10:1–4).

Both Nehemiah and Ezra had hard-hearted rebels on their hands. Nehemiah tried to soften their hearts through desperate behavior. Ezra resorted to desperate prayer. Desperate behavior resulted in temporary compliance. Desperate prayer resulted in a change of heart.

What lessons can parents draw from these two men's examples?—two very important ones. First, no amount of desperate behavior will soften a heart hard toward God. Second, the only thing that can soften a hard heart is the hand of God.

What can we do to get God to move His hand on behalf of our children? He's given us only one thing: desperate prayer.

Desperate prayer is the means we use to surrender our kids to Christ. There's nothing we do as parents that impacts their hearts more than this. Desperate prayer is most powerful when it's a parent's first choice instead of his or her last resort. We say, Anything I can do to help this kid is feeble compared to what You can do, God! The pressures on her are way too great internally, externally. There's no way that I can ever win the battle for my kid's heart if You don't intervene, God. Please.

When problems and crises arise in our kids' lives, it only makes sense to get teams of people entering into desperate prayer for them.

What surrender is not

At this point, it is important to dispel some false notions people have about the idea of "surrendering" our kids. Sometimes certain destructive attitudes are mistakenly labeled as biblical surrender.

Surrender is not **irresponsibility** on the part of the parent. It's not simply shrugging off responsibility and saying, OK, there's nothing I can do about it. She didn't come in at curfew last night. Well, God please help her come in at curfew tomorrow.

That's irresponsibility. That's not the kind of surrender we're talking about.

Surrender is not **indifference**—quite the opposite. Surrender requires desperate prayer, desperate concern. There's no way we can pray desperately about something if we're indifferent toward it. Indifferent prayers have no impact on God. It's only earnest, desperate prayers that have impact on God.

Surrender is not **resignation**: OK, God I've tried everything. I wash my hands of this kid.

That's bailing out. Parents who surrender their kids in the biblical sense stay deeply involved with them. In fact, they have more energy to parent because they are parenting from rest.

Surrender is not **giving in to the teenager**. Arnie was seventeen and had just graduated from high school. However, he wouldn't do anything his parents told him to do. He cussed at them every time they tried. For example, they asked him to put his dishes away after he finished eating. Arnie's response? He stood up and put his fist through the wall of the kitchen. His parents were afraid of him. So every night after supper Mom and Dad went upstairs and locked themselves in their bedroom, hoping Arnie would leave them alone. That's surrendering control of the home to the kid. That's not the kind of surrender we're talking about, either.

What surrender is

Surrendering our kids to the Lord Jesus Christ means we never give up caring. We never stop desperately praying for them. The harder their hearts become, the more desperate we become in our prayer—the greater the pressure we put on God. And you know what? God loves it. He's absolutely delighted when His children put the pressure they're feeling on Him. He absolutely loves it. That's what He wants us to do.

Consider what He might say: My shoulders are broad. I can handle the pressure. Don't put all that pressure on your kids. Don't fool yourself into thinking that if you could just manipulate your kid enough, or bargain with her or yell enough or lecture enough or come up with enough consequences she'd change. Don't kid yourself into thinking, either, that if you put enough pressure on yourself, you could become a perfect parent and produce a perfect kid.

No, put the pressure on Me. Cry out to Me. Tell Me, what do you want Me to do with your kid? What do you see? What's she hungry for that only I can meet? What rebellion can you see in the heart that only I can cleanse? Put the pressure on Me."

God's instruction to parents concerning surrender is simple: Turn to Me with the fear, the pressure, the confusion, the desperation that can't be avoided.

When we do that—when we surrender our kids to the Lord—we're ready to do what is the most creative aspect of the REST strategy. We're ready to teach.

As long as we are behaving desperately, we're not going to be very good teachers. Surrender frees us from desperation.

Now we can teach.

Eleven

Step Four—Teaching for Maximum Impact

Every kid is a student of his parents. By the time he becomes an independent adult, he has learned thousands of lessons about life by watching and listening to them. The lessons he has learned from them have more impact on the kind of person he decides to be than any other single influence in his life.

My son, Crying Flea

Bill signed up at the YMCA with his eleven-year-old twin sons, Mark and Steve, to participate in a father/son program known as Indian Guides. At the first meeting the "chief" of the "tribe" instructed the dads to pick Indian names for themselves and their sons. On the way home that night Bill announced what each of their Indian names would be.

"My name will be Sleeping Bull, since sleeping is what I like to do the most. And your name, Steve, is going to be Running Deer, since you're the best athlete in our family. And your name, Mark, will be Crying Flea, since all you are is a little crybaby."

True to Sleeping Bull's words, these were the names that each of them wore on their Indian vests all year.

Bill taught a life-changing lesson to Mark, all right. Recalling this painful event years later, Mark observed what

189

this experience taught him: Mask my true identity, never share my real feelings, always appear organized and in charge, never give anyone anything to criticize.

This lesson sentenced Mark to loneliness and isolation. When he graduated from college he was still unable to enter into honest, intimate relationships with others.

Frank taught an entirely different kind of lesson to his daughter.

The grouchy grandma

Every year Frank's mother came for a month-long visit. It was dreaded because of the kind of woman she was—sour, vicious, and cranky. She would spend the entire time finding someone or something to criticize. She was particularly unmerciful with the kids, especially when Frank and his wife were not around.

When Frank's oldest daughter, Joan, was ten years old, Grandma's reign of terror came to an end. Frank overheard his mother putting Joan down—calling her "a fat, ugly slob." Frank immediately intervened.

"Mom, nothing could be more untrue. Joan is a beautiful girl, and I like her just the way she is. Besides we don't speak to each other like that around our home. Although we love you very much, if you continue to speak this way, you will have to go home."

What a moment! Frank's family couldn't believe anyone could stand up to Grandma and live!

From then on, Grandma was a different person. She became almost pleasant to have around.

Years later, Joan recounted this story as one of the happiest events in her childhood. She learned many lessons that day from her father. She learned that she could trust his strength. Also, she learned there must be something beautiful about her for her dad to take such a risk to defend her. Much of the confidence and courage she displayed in reaching out to others as a high school student she attributed to the lesson she learned that day from her dad.

Kids are constantly learning from their parents. Almost everything parents say or do teaches their children important lessons about life, about themselves, and about God. Like Bill and Frank, however, parents seldom plan in advance what lessons they will teach.

Seldom are they even aware of the lessons they teach. Although it is the most influential responsibility parents have in their kids' lives, it is often the responsibility they think and plan least about.

The Apostle Paul recognized how central teaching is to parenting. In Ephesians 6:4, he admonished parents to be deliberate about the kinds of teachers they are. "Fathers, do not exasperate your children; instead bring them up in the training and instruction of the Lord."

When Paul wrote these words, he pictured a teacher quite different from today's model. Today when we speak of teachers, the picture that comes to mind is of a paid professional who instructs students in a designated place for a designated time period. This kind of teacher is foreign to the writers of the New Testament.

How the Bible characterizes teachers

When the New Testament writers referred to teachers, they were speaking of men and women with these characteristics:

Life-long commitment
The early Christian teacher's commitment to a student was not for a term, a semester, or a school year. It was for life. When a teaching relationship was established, nothing could

destroy it. The teacher was committed to stay involved with the student no matter what the cost. Notice the strength of Paul's commitment to his students in Thessalonica: "We had previously suffered and been insulted in Philippi, as you know, but with the help of our God we dared to tell you his gospel in spite of strong opposition" (1 Thess. 2:2).

Paul's commitment to his students even endured separation. When it came time for his students to separate geographically, Paul continued to teach them through visits, letters, and messengers. They would be his disciples, or students, for life.

In our culture today, where can we find this kind of commitment to students? Today's kids have grown accustomed to an endless sea of teachers drifting in and out of their lives. After a while kids become callused toward their teachers. Why should I let someone matter to me who is going to be around for such a short time?

Voluntary love

New Testament teachers never taught for pay or for personal gain. Their students never had to worry about what their motives were. Look how Paul describes his own teaching practices:

> You know we never used flattery, nor did we put on a mask to cover up greed—God is our witness. We were not looking for praise from men, not from you or anyone else.
>
> As apostles of Christ we could have been a burden to you, but we were gentle among you, like a mother caring for her little children (1 Thess. 2:5–7).

Greek and Roman schools during this period operated by a different philosophy. At these schools students had to pay for the privilege of associating with the teachers. No one ever had to pay tuition, however, to associate with Paul or Jesus.

New Testament teachers made themselves available to students out of love.

Where in today's world can kids find these kinds of teachers? As school budgets are cut, both curricular and extracurricular programs are dropped. There's no money to pay teachers, and no teachers who are willing to volunteer their time.

Perhaps kids have a right to get suspicious when nearly everyone who teaches them is getting paid for it: Do these people really care about me? Or are they just doing it to make a living?

Personal contact

New Testament teachers always got personally involved with their students. They reveled in everyday, hands-on situations with them. Again, Paul describes this in his own approach:

> We loved you so much that we were delighted to share with you not only the gospel of God but our lives as well, because you had become so dear to us. Surely you remember, brothers, our toil and hardship; we worked night and day in order not to be a burden to anyone while we preached the gospel of God to you (1 Thess. 2:8–9).

When I ride my bicycle I put on a pair of riding gloves. After a long ride, when I take my gloves off the emblem of the glove is left impressed into my skin. The very image of the glove has been pushed into my skin because of the close contact. The mark remains for hours.

New Testament teachers depended on close personal contact to leave their own images on their students. They taught them in ways that would leave marks for life.

They invited their students to live with them, work with them, eat with them, and travel with them. Their classroom was the world they lived in.

They knew that maximum impact in students' lives could only be accomplished through this kind of intense personal contact. It was of this kind of teacher and of this kind of training Jesus was speaking in Luke 6:40: "A student is not above his teacher, but everyone who is fully trained will be like his teacher."

The practice today of sending kids into impersonal and formal settings to learn from professional teachers and counselors is severely limited in the kind of impact it can have on students' lives. It can be effective at imparting information to kids. But it is ineffective at imparting values.

Shaping how a kid thinks, how he makes his decisions, what he values in life is not done effectively in formal classroom settings. This is why even traditional Sunday school programs and youth ministries are limited in the impact they can have. They are limited by the very way they are structured. They do not provide close personal contact between teachers and students.

Kids are heavily influenced by the people they are with on a continual basis. Where do our kids get the opportunity to be with adult teachers? So few do. That's why too often their most influential teachers become their own peers.

Living illustrations

The New Testament teacher always modeled in daily life the truths he taught his students. That's why Paul could challenge his student Timothy with the following words:

> You, however, know all about my teaching,
> my way of life, my purpose, faith, patience, love,
> endurance, persecutions, sufferings—what kinds

of things happened to me in Antioch, Iconium, and Lystra, the persecutions I endured. Yet the Lord rescued me from all of them. . . . But as for you, continue in what you have learned and have become convinced of, because you know those from whom you learned it (2 Tim. 3:10–11,14).

The power of Paul's teaching came from the fact that his students personally knew him and had observed him living out the very truths he wanted them to live out.

New Testament teachers always invited their students to come with them into the ordinary routine of their lives. They didn't see their students for only one hour a week in a classroom. Somebody estimated that it would take over two hundred years for a Sunday school teacher who sees his students for an hour a week to equal the amount of time Jesus spent with His disciples in three short years.

Where in our kids' world do they get the opportunity to observe their teachers living out in daily life the very truths they are teaching in the classroom? Perhaps our kids get this opportunity at summer camps, where they live with the adults who are teaching them. But it lasts only a few weeks at most. What about the rest of the year?

Concentrated attention

The New Testament teacher would commit himself only to as many students as he had time to personally know and nurture. Jesus limited this number to twelve. Where can a kid go today to get the kind of concentrated attention Paul gave his students?

For you know that we dealt with each of you as a father deals with his own children, encouraging, comforting, urging you to live lives worthy of God, who calls you into his kingdom and glory (1 Thess. 2:11–12).

Make no mistake, our kids want this kind of concentrated attention from their teachers. They thrive on it when they get it.

Where do we find teachers who are committed to stay with them for life, teachers who aren't just doing it because it's their job, teachers who roll up their sleeves and get involved personally with our kids, teachers who illustrate with their lives how our kids can live out the truth practically, teachers who aren't spread so thin that they can concentrate their attention specifically on our teens?

Parents as teachers

There's really only one place we can go today to find adults who possess the resources and position to be New Testament teachers to our kids. And that place is our homes.

Parents have the opportunity, like no one else, to be teachers in the New Testament sense to our kids. We have a relationship with them for life. We're not getting paid for it. We have personal contact with them on a daily basis. They get to observe us live out Christian truth for them in dozens of real life situations each week. And we have only a limited number of kids we have to concentrate on. We're in a natural position to be the most influential teachers they'll ever have.

Teaching for maximum impact

Since we are in such a good position to teach our kids the New Testament way, how can we take advantage of it and use it for maximum impact on them? Parents seldom plan what or how we will teach our teenagers. Instead, we end up teaching in a hit-or-miss fashion. Running aimlessly, or beating the air, as Paul described it. When we do not strategically plan the lessons we want to teach our kids there are two consequences.

First, we teach lessons to our kids that only *encourage their rebellion.*

Sally's dad had no plan

When Sally, a quiet and compliant high school junior, admitted telling a lie to her father, he didn't stop to plan what lesson Sally needed right then.

Instead he fired from the hip. He flew into a rage and took away all her privileges for a month. The lesson this taught her only reinforced her tendency to be deceptive.

She learned from her dad's reaction that it's too dangerous to let anyone see her flaws or faults. She committed herself even more to never let another person know what she was really like on the inside. In a way, she became more dishonest, going to even greater lengths to hide from others who she was and what she wanted.

There's no question Sally needed input from her parents. She needed them to teach her a biblical way to find what her heart hungered for. She needed to experience how speaking the truth in love to others offered more rewards than hiding the truth in fear did.

Inadvertently teaching her the opposite lesson was the consequence of Sally's father putting no thought into his teaching.

A second consequence of not planning is that *the lesson that needed to be taught goes untaught.*

Sally's parents lost a critical opportunity to teach their daughter the truth that could have set her free.

God is the Master Teacher. He is a master at using events of the moment to teach lessons. And He is a master at planning just the right learning experiences that will motivate us to return to the path of truth. He is deliberate, not haphazard, in the way He goes about teaching His children. "Our fathers disciplined us for a little while as they thought best; but God disciplines us for our good, that we may share in his holiness" (Heb. 12:10). In the same way, we will have maximum impact for good on our children when we become deliberate in our teaching strategy.

Five questions for maximizing our teaching

Here are five questions designed as a tool for parents of teens. As you thoughtfully and prayerfully answer them for each of your kids, you will be constructing a teaching plan that is designed for maximum impact on each of their lives. Of course, the questions presuppose that you have already spent time exploring what's going on in and around your teen.

Question #1—What kind of rebellious behavior—defiance, compliance, impotence, or negligence—is currently taking my teenager off the pathway of truth?

As we attempt to answer this question it is important that we do not settle for a one word answer. Answering it not only requires us to identify the specific brand of rebellion our teen is using (for example, in Sally's case—compliance), but it also requires us to identify all the individual behaviors that are part of her overall pattern of rebellion.

Sally's parents might have answered something like this:

Sally rebels in a compliant way. She avoids obeying God and loving others by holding her true feelings in. She chooses to do only those things that will please others. She acts like a different person at school than at home or church. She displays or exaggerates her achievements to make others pay attention to her. Sally shows little interest in what others are thinking or feeling. She refuses to talk to or associate with new people. Instead, she spends most of her free time making herself, her room, or her car appear unflawed. This way, she avoids any situation she can't control.

When we step back and look for the overall theme of our teenager's life, a lot of behaviors that previously appeared innocent or even constructive are exposed as destructive. Taking several samples of her behavior and tracing them to the common goal also gives us valuable insight into what our teen hungers for. This is what the second question focuses on.

Question #2—How is my teen's rebellious behavior satisfying his hungry heart?

We've already observed that kids do not choose their behaviors arbitrarily—especially behaviors like Sally's, that call for a great deal of energy, time, and suffering from the adolescent. Kids choose to rebel because they're starving for something, and they believe that their hunger can only be satisfied in activities found off the pathway of truth.

The task facing us in answering this question is to determine what exactly it is that our teen's behavior is designed to accomplish.

If Sally's parents had taken time to consider this they might have come to the following conclusions: Sally is starved for warmth. She has no trouble experiencing height around others. She is a stand-out in several ways, in academics, athletics, music. But none of these achievements are able to capture the human intimacy she longs for.

By packaging herself as the perfect Christian she intimidates people. Some even look at her as a snob. She certainly doesn't come across as the kind of person who needs or wants personal attention from anyone. The only warmth her compliance can get is the fleeting smile or the congratulatory pat on the back when she does something impressive. That's not enough to satisfy her hunger. Now she's resorting to hoping that another "inch"—or two—would win more warmth from others. But that's doomed to fail too.

When we get a fix on what our kids are really after, the futility of their rebellion becomes all too obvious. Rebellion is never very effective, at least not for very long, at satisfying the hunger of the human heart. Seeing this only makes us long even more for them to be liberated from their belief that rebellion is the pathway to life.

The third question asks us to consider what kind of lesson will liberate them.

Question #3—What kind of lesson will motivate my teenager to give up his rebellious behavior and get back on the pathway of truth?

Of course, the key word in this question is motivate. We cannot force our kids to be the kind of people God wants them to be. What we can do, however, is teach them about both pathways—the pathway to death and the pathway to life—and pray that God will use our teaching to motivate them to choose the pathway of life. This is the approach that Paul advocated for Timothy, and certainly the approach he would advocate for parents today.

The Lord's servant must not quarrel; instead he must be kind to everyone, able to teach, not resentful. Those who oppose him he must gently instruct, in the hope that God will grant them repentance leading them to a knowledge of the truth, and that they will come to their senses and escape from the trap of the devil, who has taken them captive to do his will (2 Tim. 2:24–26).

In answering this question, parents should attempt to put the lesson they want their kid to learn in one succinct sentence. It should contain the truth that we believe will convince him of the futility of his rebellion and of the rewards of loving obedience.

Complete this sentence

We can put the lesson into words by completing this sentence:

The lesson that will convince my son or daughter to return to the pathway of truth is _____

This is a sentence, of course, that should be completed in a different way for every teen. Each is unique in his rebellion and in his needs. And every teen needs the truth served up to him by his parents in a unique way.

If Sally's parents had followed this strategy they might have completed the sentence this way:

The lesson that will convince Sally to return to the pathway of truth is experiencing little or no warmth through performing or playacting, while experiencing her greatest warmth through offering honest parts of herself in serving Christ.

What do they experience?

Notice the emphasis in our lesson must be on what our kids experience. Adolescents are profoundly influenced by what they experience. Sally was far more influenced by what she experienced when she told her dad about her lie, than she was by what her Sunday school teacher said in last week's lesson about integrity. Sunday school teachers are limited largely to teaching by precept. Parents, however, have the resources and opportunities to teach both by precept and by experience.

The fourth question asks us to pinpoint the kind of experiences that will drive home the lesson we want to teach our kids.

Question #4—What experiences will enable my teenager to discover the lesson I want him to learn?

Learning experiences can sometimes be engineered for a teen by his parents. And sometimes they can't be. Sometimes parents can only pray for God to bring them about. Whichever is the case, it's important that parents attempt to identify the kinds of experiences their teen needs. This enables them to engineer whichever ones they can, and pray for whichever ones they can't. It also clues them in to what kind of experiences they should stand ready to welcome into their teen's life.

Learning experiences can be classified as either "push" experiences or "pull" experiences. A push experience motivates kids to be repulsed by their own rebellion. It exposes how futile their rebellious behaviors are and pushes them back toward the pathway of truth. A pull experience motivates kids to be drawn toward being voluntary lovers. It shows how rewarding life on the pathway of truth can be and pulls the kids to return to it.

Parents should seek experiences of both kinds for their kid. Certainly from the kid's perspective, pull experiences are a lot more pleasant than push experiences.

Sally's parents could have identified several experiences of both kinds that would have driven the liberating truth home to her:

Push experiences
  • People ignoring or responding indifferently toward her achievements and exaggerations of achievements.

• People giving her feedback about the way she comes across as snobbish, self-absorbed, and shallow.

• People catching her in lies or exaggerations and letting her know that this makes them feel anything but warm toward her.

Pull experiences

• Sally admitting a serious fault or flaw to others and feeling accepted by them.

• Sally being caught in a private act of kindness or caring, and being told the positive impact it has.

• Sally being recognized or sought out by others for who she is inwardly, rather than for who she is outwardly.

Any one of these experiences will go farther toward liberating Sally than a thousand words of instruction will.

When parents make a deliberate attempt like this to identify the learning experiences that would be the most liberating for their adolescent they equip themselves to parent with confidence and power.

When experiences like these occur they are prepared to help their adolescent evaluate them and draw the intended lesson from them. Often the lesson is not initially obvious to the teen.

He will need help from his parents to weigh the experience and sift out the truth. This puts him in the active role of a discoverer rather than in the passive role of a listener. And it makes his parents partners instead of preachers.

The last question helps parents identify the specific situations in which learning experiences might be engineered for their kids.

Question #5—Which situations in my teen's life will be the most conducive for learning experiences like the ones I listed above?

When parents identify in advance the situations that are most conducive for learning they will be more alert and prepared to take advantage of them when they occur. Sally's parents lost a critical opportunity to teach their daughter when she volunteered information to them about one of her own flaws.

Missed opportunities to teach

Here's a list of other situations which Sally's parents could have utilized for learning had they planned in advance:

• When Sally came home with her grades or an award for her achievements (conducive for a push experience).

• When Sally failed at something or some flaw of hers was exposed (conducive for a pull experience).

• When Sally changed her looks (conducive for a push experience).

• When Sally was honest or open about something she was thinking or feeling (conducive for a pull experience).

Every one of these situations affords an opportunity for Sally's parents to either observe or engineer one or more of the learning experiences that we listed when answering question number four.

Using these questions to construct a teaching strategy can be one of the most stimulating and beneficial things parents can do for their kids. It certainly incorporates the elements of creativity, imagination, and planning that good parenting requires. And it involves parents in a tangible way with God in the holy task of guiding an adolescent toward the pathway of truth.

Twelve

Rod, Louise, and Gary: A Case Study

The two of us are, between us, fathers of seven teenagers; it is often difficult to know how to rest. It's difficult to believe that when Jesus said, "Come to me, all of you who are weary and burdened, and I will give you rest (Matt. 11:28), He was speaking to parents of teens, too. All of us need help to know what it means to rest.

The preceding four chapters detailed each step of the REST strategy. In this chapter, we'll show how two parents applied these four steps when they were confronted with a unique set of teenage problems. This is the REST strategy in action.

Gary's defiance started in junior high

Rod and Louise were parents of a seventeen-year-old son named Gary. Gary had been growing increasingly defiant since entering adolescence. The defiant behavior started in junior high when he grew physically larger than his dad. That's when he started to talk back to his mother and father and ignore their instructions.

The same behavior spread to school. Gary was soon receiving suspensions for his defiance and disrespect with teachers. Since Rod pastors a prominent church, he was embarrassed over his son's growing reputation.

Rod responded with a get tough approach, which led to angry confrontations with his son. He withdrew most of Gary's privileges. Gary remained grounded on most weekends throughout his first two years of high school. Occasionally, he would temporarily comply with the rules just to get his dad off his back.

Eleventh grade explosion

During his junior year, things finally exploded. Early one morning, Gary was arrested at school. He had sneaked out of the house around midnight, met a few other boys, and started drinking. They decided to break into the school. Around 2 a.m., they were caught in the act of spray-painting graffiti on the walls. All of the boys were intoxicated at the time of the arrest. The police estimated the damage in the thousands of dollars.

This seemed like the last straw to Rod when he got the call at home. He refused to go to the police station.

"I want him to stay locked up for a long time," Rod told the officer.

This triggered quite an argument between Rod and Louise. She finally went to the police station and bailed Gary out herself, which further enraged Rod.

"You can bail him out, but he's not coming back here," said Rod. Louise quickly arranged for Gary to stay with friends of the family.

Up to this time, Rod had never stopped to reflect on his relationship with his son, nor had he considered that his parenting approach could be contributing to Gary's rebellion. The pressure on Rod to make Gary comply and appear healthy had been enormous. Since he had failed at this, he didn't want anything more to do with his son. He refused his wife's suggestions to attend counseling sessions with Gary.

Would Rod lose his pastorate?

For Rod, there was no rest or peace in avoiding his son. He could justify his angry feelings and punitive actions, but he couldn't shake the depression that set in. Feelings of worthlessness and loneliness enshrouded him. The situation impaired his ability to carry out his responsibilities as a pastor. The fear that he would lose his position finally motivated him to go to some Christian men and women he respected.

Wisely, these people encouraged Rod to reflect on his own hungry heart.

Rod resisted this at first. He wanted action! He wanted a formula that would turn Gary back into the sweet, responsive kid he was in elementary school.

But his friends kept insisting he take a look at himself, first. They knew Rod was like a raging sea on the inside. Until the sea was stilled he would be unable to be the kind of dad Gary needed.

Reflection was hard

Reflection was difficult for Rod. He said he seldom did it because it only made him angry. When his friends asked him to explain his feelings, he told them he'd been disappointed a lot by others.

With a little encouragement, Rod began to talk about events he'd never talked about before. He'd grown up in a family in which he always felt inferior to his brothers. He felt he'd never gotten any breaks or recognition. He was never the one who got the medal. As a teenager, his heart ached to be reassured that he wasn't a failure.

All his life he had hungered to get in a position where everybody—his parents, his wife, his kids, the whole community—finally recognized how valuable he was. Now he felt this could never be accomplished because he had a son who delighted in making him look like a total failure.

Rod's friends sat astounded. Not only were they seeing Rod's hungry heart, but they were also seeing his wicked heart. Rod was trying to achieve height in the eyes of all those around him, while ignoring the high position he already held in God's eyes as one of His children. Rod's friends stopped him and pointed out that by demanding that people in his world give him his height, he wasn't loving or serving them at all. He was using them, and even abusing them if they made him look small.

When Rod's friends pointed this out, he did not enjoy it at all. However, he listened and began to understand what it was that came between him and his family. He began to see, too, that it was neither possible nor desirable to attain the height he hungered for from anyone but Christ. All this reflection on himself began to make Rod that much more curious about Gary. If I'm starving for height, I wonder what Gary's starving for?—was a question Rod never considered before.

With help from his friends, Rod decided to explore what was going on in his son's life. He knew he had to rebuild their relationship. Observation, listening, and questioning were tools that could only be used at close range.

Rod starts exploring with Louise

Rod knew Louise was spending time with Gary, and had a lot of opportunity to observe what was going on with him. The first step Rod took to get to know his son was to ask Louise to share all of her observations about him. Louise felt eager to do this, thrilled at Rod's new interest in Gary. She had spent a lot of time thinking about her son and her husband, and was an important source of information for Rod.

In the last few years she had been unable to talk to Rod much about Gary. Any such talk triggered so much anger in him that she chose to keep her thoughts to herself. But now she was experiencing a changed husband. She could talk to him without him getting upset or racing away.

Before, he was afraid to hear bad news about his family because it made him feel small. Personal reflection helped him see this and decide he wanted to be different. He asked Christ to help him know the truth about his family and to give him the strength to deal with whatever he found.

Louise pointed out that her son's defiance had been seriously curbed since he had moved in with their friends. The feedback she was getting from this family was that, for the most part, he was being cooperative and obedient. Even the school officials reported that Gary seemed to be better behaved, although he still ran with a group of kids that were known for their wild parties.

This led her to believe that his rebellion had a lot to do with his relationship with them. She told Rod that it almost seemed that he was mad at them for something—out for revenge. Now that he had publicly embarrassed them his vendetta seemed satisfied. When she was with him he was a lot more relaxed.

Time for Gary to come home

She knew the solution to his problems was not to keep him in someone else's home. But she was afraid if they brought him home, he would resume his more destructive behaviors.

With Louise's encouragement, Rod began to spend Saturday afternoons with his son. Gary wasn't too excited about the idea at first. However, he agreed just for curiosity's sake.

At first Rod wisely chose just to play with his son—golf and tennis mostly. This put him in a position to observe Gary and to listen to him. It was the first time Rod could remember ever just listening to his son.

Before things blew up Rod had always done most of the talking. Rarely did they play together. The time they spent together had been strictly for work—at home, at church, even at school.

Rod volunteered for a few years as a coach on his son's football team and had worked extensively with Gary on the fundamentals of the game. He remembered being very disappointed with Gary when he didn't want to go out for football again his junior year. He couldn't even remember the reason Gary gave for not continuing, if he even gave one at all.

As Rod thought back over these events he wondered if they might be connected to the anger in Gary that Louise observed.

It didn't take long for Rod and Gary to start looking forward to their Saturday afternoons together. A friendship began to develop. Soon Gary was letting down the walls and talking freely around his father.

This was a mixed blessing for Rod. He was happy Gary was talking. However, it was hard for Rod because he heard a lot of things that concerned him greatly. He heard opinions and values that were not Christian at all. He sensed, though, it was too soon to start teaching his son.

He knew he had to explore more first in order to understand what was at the bottom of Gary's rebellion.

Rod began to develop skill at asking Gary questions and drawing him out. In time, Gary began to talk about his anger. In bits and pieces the story began to emerge in unexpected ways. One time at a bowling alley Gary called his dad's attention to the trophy cabinet.

"That's how I felt growing up, just like one of those trophies." Fortunately, Rod followed up the comment with a probing question, "That had to be awful. What do you remember about it?"

Another time when they were riding somewhere in the car and saw a high school football team practicing, Gary commented, "Dad, I bet you wish you were out on that field right now coaching a star, don't you?" Again, Rod responded with a question that invited Gary to share what he was thinking. "What makes you think that, Gary?"

Exploration became enjoyable

Exploration wasn't nearly as difficult or laborious as Rod originally thought it would be. In fact, it was enjoyable, even exciting, to spend time with his son and learn what really made him tick. The more he learned about Gary, the easier it was to forgive him for his rebellion to and offer him friendship.

In a matter of weeks, Rod had acquired some substantial insight into his son. The clues were there all along, but somehow Rod had missed them. He knew his own preoccupation with making a name for himself and becoming a standout in Christian circles had made him blind to anybody else's needs but his own. But now reflection and exploration had taken the blinders off.

Why Gary was angry

Of course Gary was angry. Here was a kid who was created by God to rule the universe, to wield real power, to make a difference in his world. However, the message he constantly heard from his dad and mom was, Don't rock the boat or make any waves. Don't be your own person. Instead, be our trophy. Stand wherever we place you and just shine.

Gary recalled trying so hard to shine like he was supposed to. He wanted to be the Christian trophy his dad and mom wanted him to be. Both at church and school he always tried to do and say only the things that would reflect positively on them.

But as Gary moved into junior high school he came to realize that being a Christian trophy had some severe drawbacks. Nobody took you seriously. Everybody saw you as weak. People—even your own parents—ignored you because you were so good and never made any waves

When Gary was in eighth grade his dad and mom decided to move across the country without even asking his opinion. In ninth grade his dad decided Gary should play football and volunteered to help coach Gary's team. In tenth grade his dad decided that Gary should break the school record for total tackles in a season. All this time Gary was growing more and more resentful over the lack of control he had over his own life and activities. And when he failed to break the tackle record, after his dad had bragged publicly that he would, he felt humiliated.

Defiance gave Gary weight

Gary was starving for "weight." He felt that his thoughts, desires, and opinions carried no weight with his parents. He also believed that giving in any longer to their pressure to be a model Christian son would prevent him from having any weight among his friends at school.

Defiance helped him feel strong. Rocking the boat for his parents made him feel powerful. And earning the right to live on his own—the way he perceived his living situation—was the ultimate way he could to prove he was weightier, more powerful, than his parents. Gary believed that he could only feel powerful if he lived off the pathway of truth.

Time to surrender

When Rod and Louise came to understand the pressures behind their son's rebellion, they were filled with both compassion and alarm. Desperately they wanted to help him get back on the pathway of truth—and experience the weight he could have as a servant of Christ. They knew that eventually the weight he felt through his defiance would evaporate as he became an independent adult. They wanted him see this more than they had ever wanted anything else for him. But never had they felt more helpless and inadequate to accomplish something.

Rod and Louise knew it was time to surrender. Together they brought their desperation to Christ and poured it out to Him in prayer. How their son's defiance made them look in front of others didn't even seem to be an issue any longer. The only thing that seemed important was Gary acquiring a new heart. And this they knew was beyond their ability to pull off. It was entirely in God's hands now. Only He possessed the ability to transform their son from the inside. They prayed with the same earnestness they would if they had received news that their son was dying of AIDS.

Desperate prayer

But Rod and Louise's prayers were not just focused on Gary. They prayed with the same desperation for their own hearts. They knew their own hunger and wickedness had played a big role in encouraging Gary's departure from the pathway of truth. Now they wanted to be used by God to call him back— to call him to compassion, not to compliance. And that required a change of their own hearts. It was another first: Rod and Louise knelt beside their bed, asking God to satisfy their hungry hearts and fill them with love for Gary, and for others.

It had been four months now since Gary had moved out of the house. It took that long for Rod and Louise to surrender him to Christ. They knew, though, the pressure they felt to make him behave would quickly return unless they continued to surrender him to Christ on a daily basis.

They knew now it was time to bring Gary home. Their opportunities to teach him would be too limited as long as he was living elsewhere. Besides, his independence from them was only serving to reinforce his notion that rebellion against God was the only way to feel powerful.

Would Gary come home?

They knew, however, that a decision to have him live at home again would not sit well with him. It would probably trigger a new round of rebellious behaviors. But this is part of what they had to surrender to God. They had to surrender their reputations, their right to have a harmonious home, and the time that parenting a rebellious son would no doubt require.

They were right. Gary was not excited about moving home. He put up little active resistance at first, though. The way his parents were acting these days puzzled him more than it enraged him. They continued to listen more than they lectured. They didn't seem to sweat the small stuff any more. They acted like his opinions mattered, and discussed decisions with him before they were made. Little did he realize that his parents were teaching him an important lesson without putting it into words. They were teaching him that he is a weighty person, by virtue of who he is, not on the basis of what he does.

The defiance resurfaces

At first these changes went a long way to relieve Gary's need to go off the pathway of truth to satisfy his hungry heart. But ultimately they still weren't enough. After a few weeks he decided he didn't like sharing power with his parents. He liked how it felt when he had all the power. So he fell back into his defiant behaviors again, just to remind them that even with their new strategy they couldn't make him be somebody he didn't want to be.

The resurfacing of these behaviors, of course, alarmed Rod and Louise. But they were more prepared than they'd ever been to cope with them. With most of the pressure placed on God's shoulders, they decided it was time to teach Gary something about the ultimate cost of rebellion. Up to this time they had allowed him to function as an ignorant rebel, having little awareness of the significance of his actions. In the past they had always stopped short of "wounding" him out of fear—fear of conflict, fear of public embarrassment, fear of losing their trophy.

But these were fears they were now willing to face, since they had surrendered their home, their reputations, and their son to Christ.

The warning "roar"

Even before Gary started to show outward signs again of defiance, Rod and Louise began to discuss with him the cost of living off the pathway of truth. They called to his attention the ways they saw him trying to feel powerful. They expressed concern about this and helped him visualize the long-term consequences. They urged him to consider the weight a life of service to Christ could give. In these ways they were giving their son a roar of warning.

Time to "wound"

Gary chose to ignore the roar, believing that the benefits of rebellion far outweighed the costs. He began to ignore curfews and refused to do household chores. Desperately, Rod and Louise turned again to God in prayer. They prayed for wisdom to choose a response that would be most effective in teaching Gary the significance of his rebellion. They knew it was time to wound their son out of love.

In the past, lectures, scolding, and grounding had done little to make Gary stop and think about what he was doing. They also knew that arranging for him to live with friends only added to his illusion of power. As they prayed, they wondered what kind of response on their part would capture his attention. Gary needed to get a taste now of what a lifestyle of defiance would eventually reap for him.

As Rod and Louise prayerfully considered their choices, they carefully selected the lesson they wanted to teach Gary: The longer a person lives off the pathway of truth, the harder it will be to have the kind of weight that counts. Getting clearly in mind the lesson they wanted to teach helped them to stay in the role of teachers. It also gave them a specific objective to pray about.

Teaching from a lesson plan

Having selected the truth they wanted to teach Gary, they next developed their lesson plan. They knew the plan had to provide some sample experiences for him, samples to show how defiance reaps a loss of power and samples to show how obedience reaps an increase in power. Designing these experiences took several long discussions and a lot of prayer.

They finally agreed on the following lesson plan.

Push experiences—To give Gary a taste of how defiance reduces his weight in the world, they decided to:

• Treat him matter-of-factly when he fails to obey, or obeys in a half-hearted manner. This ruled out any pleading, lecturing, or showing of emotion in response to Gary's defiance.

• Terminate all his employment, salaries, and accompanying benefits until he applies to get them back and passes a rigorous interview. This means his defiance and irresponsibility, after one warning, will immediately result in the loss of his job as a full-time student, and all of his jobs at home. He will no longer be permitted to go to school, to help with household chores, or to clean up his room, without applying for these positions again. Meanwhile, he will lose all salary and benefits—allowances, free use of family cars, access to prepared meals, free rides, free use of telephone. Room and medical care will be the only benefits provided as long as his defiance continues.

• Immediately report to the police any illegal activities that are observed, including drinking, violation of curfews, or trespassing. If Gary chooses not to live under the authority of his parents, this will insure that he will encounter an authority that outweighs him, an authority that has the power to subdue him.

Pull experiences—To give Gary a taste of how obedience, accompanied by love, increases his weight in the world they decided to:

• Call attention to any action or choice on his part that reflects voluntary love, pointing out the positive impact it is having on others.

• Regularly ask him to move out of his safety zone and love others in ways that are difficult or dangerous for him. These will be designed to teach him two things: How much weight he can have with others when he loves them, and how little he is capable of loving others without a personal relationship with Christ.

• Invite him, on a weekly basis, to spend time with both his parents, continuing the give-and-take pattern Rod began with him on Saturday afternoons.

With their plan established, Rod and Louise felt ready to proceed. Implementing it was another act of surrender. Of course, they had no idea how Gary would react. But they knew controlling or even predicting his response was not their job. Their job was to teach. God's job was to protect their family and transform their son's heart.

When Rod and Louise matter-of-factly explained to Gary that they were going to "fire" him from all his jobs unless they saw a marked improvement within two days, he was stunned. His first response was, "You can't do that!"

"Sure we can," they retorted. "We own the company."

The approach was important

What probably confused Gary the most was the way his parents announced their intentions. They weren't the least bit unfriendly. They seemed concerned but calm. He sort of liked them this way, although he would never tell them.

Gary decided not to call their bluff yet. He knew by their tone that they were serious. He decided that if he gave it a couple of weeks, they would forget, and things would return to normal. Rod and Louise knew that their son's compliance was just the lull before the storm.

Gary tests Rod and Louise

After about two weeks, Gary decided not to come home one day after school. He missed supper without calling and came in several hours past his school night curfew. Rod and Louise said very little to him as he hurried to his bedroom. The next morning, however, Gary came down to breakfast to find his parents gone and a note waiting for him on the kitchen table. The note read:

> Dear Gary,
>
> We were sad to learn about your decision yesterday to ignore our warnings and disobey our instructions. You will have to prepare your own breakfast this morning since you have lost your privileges to eat prepared meals with your family.
>
> By the way, you are fired. Don't bother to complete any of the work you were supposed to do yesterday. We have given all your household jobs to your sister, along with your allowance. She'll be

cleaning and picking up your room from now on, too. We have given her permission to keep for herself anything she finds lying on the floor.

Don't get alarmed when you go outside and discover that the car we had provided for you is gone. We decided to sell it. It's a family car, you know, one of the fringe benefits of working for us.

We'll be out running errands for a while. We have to go by the school to let them know we're withdrawing you. Paid tuition to a private school is another fringe benefit.

You'll have to enroll yourself in public high school if you want to continue your education.

Don't go too far from home today, though. Your probation officer may be wanting to talk to you. We'll be going to see him after we finish at the school. We want him to know how you've been disregarding our curfews and failing to do your school work.

By the way, please don't use the telephone, either— another fringe benefit. We changed our phone number and now it takes a special code to use it. We're only giving the code out to those who work for us.

We should be home around 3:00 this afternoon.

Dad wants to know if you want to play tennis then. He was hoping to get in a good match before dinner.

We love you.
Dad and Mom.

Gary couldn't wait for his parents to get home that afternoon. He begged them to reconsider their actions. Rod and

Louise, however, said they would only reconsider if he gave them a written application telling them why he wanted his jobs back, and what they could expect from him if they gave them back. They told him he would have to go through a rigorous interview as well.

From ignorant rebel to subdued rebel

Within a week Gary was able to get his jobs back, but this time on his parents' terms. It took a month to get the use of a car again. Rod and Louise were pleased to see Gary approaching his responsibilities with a new sense of appreciation and care. They knew it was only the first step, though. Their teaching plan had helped their son move from being an ignorant rebel to becoming a subdued rebel. But a lot still had to happen for him to become a brokenhearted rebel.

Rod and Louise's teaching plan called for providing pull experiences for their son, as well as push experiences. One of these involved calling on Gary to love others in ways that were uncomfortable for him. As with any teenage rebel, love was quite a foreign experience for him. Seldom did he volunteer to do anything for another person. Most of the time he was too absorbed with his own needs to be interested in anybody else's.

The big storm

Rod and Louise were perplexed with how they could help Gary get a taste of what it meant to love another person selflessly. Once again they prayed to God for an opportunity to provide this learning experience for their son. That's when the big storm hit.

The heaviest rainfall ever to hit their part of the country occurred. The call went out on the radio for volunteers. Help was needed to sandbag dikes and strengthen them against the rising floodwater.

Although Rod's neighborhood was not in the threatened areas, he asked Gary to go with him and help with the sandbagging. Gary agreed. It didn't even occur to Rod that this was the very learning experience he'd been seeking for Gary.

It turned out to be the most challenging and rewarding experience of Gary's life. He and his dad labored in the storm for the better part of two days, side by side with people they'd never met before, people from a completely different socio-economic level. And they were able to save dozens of homes from being destroyed. In the end the families in the affected areas threw a victory celebration to thank all those who helped save their homes. Gary became a favorite among them since he was the youngest volunteer.

Rod and Louise used the opportunity to talk to Gary about the kind of impact his self-sacrifice had. Gary was visibly moved. For the first time he tasted the fruits of self-sacrifice and love. It was more satisfying, and weightier, than anything else he'd ever done.

Gary goes to camp

Gary began to talk about pursuing a career in which he could help others the way he helped the flood victims. Rod suggested that he volunteer on the grounds crew at a nearby camp for disadvantaged children. Gary eagerly applied and was accepted to work there for the summer.

Rod and Louise spent a lot of time in prayer the day their son left for camp. They prayed that his desire to help others would continue to grow and be encouraged over the summer. They prayed that, more importantly, God would use the camp to bring him to a point of spiritual desperation, that somehow he would come to realize how inadequate he was to love without help from Christ.

When Gary got to camp his job assignment was changed. Because there weren't enough counselors, he was asked to be in charge of a cabin of inner city junior high students. The idea seemed novel and exciting at first. But soon he discovered just how difficult it is to work with kids from such underprivileged homes. By the second day he had a full-scale revolt on his hands. The kids in his cabin wouldn't listen to a thing he said.

Frustration, fighting—and a brokenhearted rebel

Finally, out of frustration, Gary lost it himself. He challenged one of the ringleaders to fight him if he was so tough. A flurry of punches were thrown and the young boy fell to the floor bleeding and crying. As soon as Gary saw what he'd done, he felt heartsick. He attempted to apologize and give first aid, but the boy wanted to be left alone. For the next twenty-four hours none of the boys in the cabin would talk to Gary or even look at him. Gary felt very small. He wished he could die. For the first time that he could remember he prayed to God and asked Him for help.

By the end of the week Gary was at the point of quitting and going home. He couldn't believe what he had done. He told the camp director, who didn't act very concerned. He just told Gary to try to control himself better with the new group of guys that were due to arrive in a day or two. He said that these kinds of things happened to every counselor at one time or another over the summer.

The director's words did little to comfort him. He kept replaying in his mind the look on the boys' faces when he lost it in front of them. He didn't want to hurt a new group of boys that way. He was scared that he might not be able to keep the same thing from happening again.

Tears from dad—and son

Gary decided to call his Dad and ask him to come get him. After he explained to him everything that happened, he got a response from him that he didn't expect at all. He expected Rod to get mad, lecture him, maybe tell him how stupid he was. Instead, Rod wept.

Gary couldn't remember his dad ever crying before. Just the sound of it made him weep, too. In tears, Rod told his son how much he loved him and how much he appreciated his telling him what had happened. Rod went on to explain that he was crying more for joy than sadness. That confused Gary. "Why would something like this bring you joy?"

"I feel joy, son, because I hear something I've never heard before in your words. I hear brokenness. I hear a man that is honest enough to admit that there's something wrong with him."

Gary had to admit that was how he was feeling. But he still couldn't understand why it made his dad so happy.

"Gary, I've been praying for a long time that you would come to this point, that you would come to see how much you need Jesus Christ to do a work in your heart before you can be the loving man you want to be."

"But, Dad, I can't stay here and work with these kids. I'll just blow up and hurt one of them again. I know I will. Won't you come get me?"

"No, son, I'm not going to come and get you this week. I want you to stay there and work with those kids for at least one more week. Next weekend, if you're feeling the same way you're feeling now, I'll come and get you."

"Don't you understand, Dad, I can't do this. I'll just hurt them again."

"I think you're right, Gary. You don't have what it takes to love those kids on your own. The only way you'll be able to help them instead of hurt them is with God's help. Gary, have you ever asked Christ to give you a new heart?"

The son surrenders

That afternoon on the telephone Rod told his son how much a personal relationship with Christ had changed his own heart. Then they prayed together for Christ to do a work in both of them. It was the first time Gary ever came to God as a brokenhearted rebel.

Christ did not disappoint Rod or his son that week. The group of kids Gary had in his cabin were every bit as difficult to love as those in the first week. But Gary now had a resource he didn't possess the first week. He had Christ working in his heart to give him love, patience, and strength he had never experienced before. Gary experienced life as a transformed rebel. It was no surprise to Rod that his son ended up staying on at camp for the whole summer. Or that when he came home he could tell story after story of how God enabled him to have an impact on the lives of the boys who were in his cabin.

Although Rod and Louise had the privilege of watching Christ transform their son's life, that wasn't the end of their story, nor was it the end of their job as parents. In the years that followed, they continued to face numerous challenges in parenting Gary. At times he drifted into rebellion again. When he did, they found themselves starting over with him at stage one as an ignorant rebel. They had to make a deliberate decision each time to REST as they parented him. Although Gary's needs and behaviors changed as he matured, they always came back to the REST strategy as the anchor that kept them on the biblical path of parenting.

Note to the Reader

The publisher invites you to share your response to the message of this book by writing Discovery House Publishers, P. O. Box 3566, Grand Rapids, MI 49501, U.S.A. or by calling 800-653-8333. For information about other Discovery House publications, contact us at the same address and phone number.